BEHIND
THE LOST
SYMBOL

BEHIND
THE LOST
SYMBOL

The Unauthorized
Guide to Dan Brown's
Bestselling Novel

Tim Collins

BERKLEY BOOKS, NEW YORK

THE BERKLEY PUBLISHING GROUP
Published by the Penguin Group
Penguin Group (USA) Inc.
375 Hudson Street, New York, New York 10014, USA
Penguin Group (Canada), 90 Eglinton Avenue East, Suite 700, Toronto, Ontario M4P 2Y3, Canada
(a division of Pearson Penguin Canada Inc.)
Penguin Books Ltd., 80 Strand, London WC2R 0RL, England
Penguin Group Ireland, 25 St. Stephen's Green, Dublin 2, Ireland (a division of Penguin Books Ltd.)
Penguin Group (Australia), 250 Camberwell Road, Camberwell, Victoria 3124, Australia
(a division of Pearson Australia Group Pty. Ltd.)
Penguin Books India Pvt. Ltd., 11 Community Centre, Panchsheel Park, New Delhi—110 017, India
Penguin Group (NZ), 67 Apollo Drive, Rosedale, North Shore 0632, New Zealand
(a division of Pearson New Zealand Ltd.)
Penguin Books (South Africa) (Pty.) Ltd., 24 Sturdee Avenue, Rosebank, Johannesburg 2196,
South Africa

Penguin Books Ltd., Registered Offices: 80 Strand, London WC2R 0RL, England

The publisher does not have any control over and does not assume any responsibility for author or third-party websites or their content.

PRINTING HISTORY
Michael O'Mara Books trade edition / November 2009
Berkley trade paperback edition / March 2010

Library of Congress Cataloging-in-Publication Data

Collins, Tim, 1975–
   Behind the lost symbol : the unauthorized guide to Dan Brown's bestselling novel /
Tim Collins. — 1st ed.
      p.   cm.
   Includes bibliographical references.
   ISBN 978-0-425-23721-2
   1. Brown, Dan, 1964– Lost symbol—Handbooks, manuals, etc.   I. Title.
   PS3552.R685434L67335   2010
   813'.54—dc22   2009046929

PRINTED IN THE UNITED STATES OF AMERICA

10 9 8 7 6 5 4 3 2 1

CONTENTS

ACKNOWLEDGMENTS

Thanks to Collette for putting up with all my speculation about the plot of *The Lost Symbol*. Thanks also to Toby Buchan, Louise Dixon, Judith Palmer, Dominique Enright, Lesley Levene, Abi Morgan and everyone at Michael O'Mara Books for their help with this project. Finally, my thanks to David Woodroffe for the specially commissioned illustrations, Glen Saville for the U.K. cover design, and Ron Callow of Design 23 for the original design and layout of the text and plates. Thanks also to the team at Berkley for their work on the U.S. edition.

FACT

In 2009, an editor at Doubleday received a highly confidential Word document. The document was so eagerly anticipated that online forums had been speculating about its contents for six years.

All the rituals, science and organizations discussed in the document were accurate. Sort of.

This document was *The Lost Symbol*, the sequel to *The Da Vinci Code*.

INTRODUCTION

Like many people, I finally got hold of Dan Brown's third Robert Langdon novel on the morning of Tuesday, September 15, 2009. My local bookshop had opened early for the event, and quite a few people were in line to get the book, although mercifully none of them was dressed as a character from the series (I considered sporting the Robert Langdon mullet from the movie of *The Da Vinci Code*, but thought better of it).

The Lost Symbol, like its two predecessors in the Langdon series, is a fast-paced thriller that weaves fact and alternative history to expose shocking revelations about the world we think we know. It's probably fair to say that if this was a debut novel, it would have been warmly received by genre fans, and perhaps gained some mainstream media attention. But coming as the sequel to one of the bestselling novels in history, and with a record-breaking initial print run of 6.5 million copies, *The Lost Symbol* has attracted blanket media coverage, sparking critical debate and a grisly discounted cover-price war.

The Da Vinci Code was unquestionably the publishing phenomenon of the past few years, and has now sold more than 81 million copies worldwide. A huge backlash inevitably followed, and Brown became a popular target for authors and literary critics. Salman Rushdie even went as far as to describe *The Da Vinci Code* as "a novel so bad it gives bad novels a bad name." And while it would be hard to deny that Brown's prose style is simple . . .

With lots of short sentences. In italics.

. . . his novels undoubtedly work as the ruthlessly addictive blockbusters they're intended to be. But there's more to Brown's success than the simple guilty pleasure, of course. He has a gift for weaving complex ideas into his accessible prose. As Michael Baigent and Richard Leigh were so keen to remind everyone around the time of their unsuccessful plagiarism lawsuit, there was nothing especially new about the idea of the Jesus bloodline, and the theories have been doing the rounds with conspiracy buffs for years. But in Brown's hands the ideas touched a nerve worldwide and inspired fierce condemnation from Catholic groups that created endless free publicity.

The success of *The Da Vinci Code* inspired leagues of copycat authors, and the "conspiracy theory thriller" became a crowded subgenre. Titles such as *The Alexander Cipher, The Mozart Conspiracy, The Moses Stone, The Machiavelli Covenant, The Mosaic Crimes, The Templar Legacy* and *The Exodus Quest* began to appear as the bandwagon rolled on. Brown had established a formula that was easy to replicate, where a conspiracy involving a famous artist, historical figure or artifact would be unveiled in short chapters. Typically, a bizarre murder would trigger a breathless chase narrative in which a knowledgeable (but surprisingly fit) protagonist discovers a secret revealing how everything we think we know is wrong.

In the run-up to the release of *The Lost Symbol*, the online magazine *Slate* even published a Dan Brown generator, which lets you select a city and an organization and then generates the synopsis of a novel with a title like *The Forgotten Crypt*, *The Hidden Enigma* or *The Last Mausoleum*.

Perhaps to distance himself from his army of imitators, Brown has Langdon explicitly deny that he's an expert in conspiracy theories in Chapter 30 of *The Lost Symbol*. Some of the anti-Masonic theories that fans might have expected Brown to exploit, such as the inverted pentagram in the street plan above the White House, are dismissed by Langdon. Others, like the appearance of the word "Mason" on the Great Seal of the United States, are used as deliberate red herrings.

While Langdon might not be keen on the phrase "conspiracy theory," there's no denying that the novel is packed with alternative history, pseudoscience and esoterica. Brown has always been interested in creating a hybrid of lecture and thriller, but the lessons come thicker and faster than before in *The Lost Symbol* (hardly surprising when you consider that he researched it for six years). No sooner has Langdon touched down in Washington, D.C., than we're learning about Masonic Founding Fathers, Utopianism, Noetic Science, quantum mysticism and the lost wisdom of the ancients. There are even references to things we're supposed to have retained from the previous novels, such as the Rosicrucians, the Knights

Templar and the Illuminati. The effect is at times akin to dashing through a series of alternative history lectures without ever having the time to stop and listen to them.

In short, there's never been a Dan Brown novel more in need of an explanatory guide than *The Lost Symbol*. In this one, you'll find entries giving the background to Brown's book laid out in an A–Z format. Many of the facts that Dan Brown cites in his novel are solid, but there are places where he's embellished and exaggerated things to serve his storytelling, and I'll try to highlight these.

This guide serves as a primer to the complex mesh of facts and theories that make up the fictional world that I should probably resist calling "the Browniverse." Brown's skill might be to bring order from the chaos of history, religion, science and mathematics he throws at the reader, but I hope you'll agree that the chaos deserves a closer look.

Ancient Mysteries

Before the publication of *The Lost Symbol*, many Freemasons were worried that Dan Brown would portray their organization as a sinister cabal bent on world domination. In fact, Robert Langdon dismisses these kinds of theories early on in the novel. But there is one alternative history of Freemasonry that seems to have caught Brown's imagination, which is the idea that the fraternity are guardians of powerful arcane knowledge known as the "Ancient Mysteries."

In Chapter 30 of *The Lost Symbol*, Robert Langdon tells Director Sato of the legend that the powerful secret wisdom of the ancients has survived, and was protected by secret fraternities. By the early sixteenth century, Langdon explains, these groups had been wiped out by religious oppressors, and the Freemasons were the last surviving guardians. Fearing that they too would fall victim to persecution, the Masons transported this secret wisdom to the new world of America.

The theory draws on a tradition of writing about the ancient roots of Freemasonry that dates back to the oldest surviving Masonic document, *The Regius Manuscript*, a 794-line poem from around 1390, which claims that Masonry can be traced to ancient Egypt, where Euclid was the first Master Mason.

When the Reverend James Anderson published *The Constitutions of the Free-Masons* in 1723 (often known as *The Book of Constitutions*), he included a fanciful history of Masonry that embraced the builders and mathematicians of Rome, Greece and Egypt. Since then, writers like Arthur Edward Waite, Eliphas Lévi and Manly P. Hall have written thick books detailing how the roots of Masonry are in the Mystery Schools of Egypt, the Kabbalah and ancient books of magic. The genre has even had a contribution from Founding Father Thomas Paine, who wrote a paper about how Masonry developed from the ancient druids called *An Essay on the Origin of Free-Masonry*.

Dan Brown seems to have been especially influenced by Manly P. Hall, and *The Lost Symbol* fittingly begins with a quotation from Hall's magnum opus, *The Secret Teachings of All Ages: An Encyclopedic Outline of Masonic, Hermetic, Qabbalistic and Rosicrucian Symbolical Philosophy*. In this densely written tome, which was published in 1928 when Hall was just twenty-seven years old, he traces things such as the Kabbalah, alchemy, the Mystery Schools and Rosicrucianism back to Freemasonry. He proposes that Freemasons are the guardians of the wisdom of the ancients, which they have veiled from the uninitiated through a complex web of symbolism.

Given his interest in the mystical aspects of Freemasonry, it's no surprise that Dan Brown decided to focus on the Scottish Rite, an appendant body that has a history of proclaiming ancient roots. It was originally inspired by Andrew Michael Ramsay, a Scottish-born author who lived in France in the eighteenth century. Ramsay claimed that Freemasonry was descended from mystical orders and transported to Europe by crusading medieval knights. These ideas captured the imagination of French Masons, who devised hundreds of additional degrees based on them.

The notion that Freemasonry has ancient roots was further embellished by Albert Pike when he rewrote the Scottish Rite in 1868. Pike was heavily influenced by French occultist Eliphas Lévi, who believed that Freemasonry was derived from pagan mysticism, alchemy, Kabbalism, Gnosticism and the religions of ancient Egypt.

When considering Pike's version of the Scottish Rite, it's worth remembering that his sources were the inventions of Ramsay and Lévi, as well as the fertile imaginations of French Freemasons, so it can't be taken as evidence of a link between the Masons and the ancients.

The idea of Freemasons guarding the lost wisdom of the ages clearly excited Dan Brown, and the untapped potential of humanity hinted at in the Ancient Mysteries and Noetic Science is a key theme in *The Lost Symbol*, but it shouldn't come as a surprise to learn that these mystical theories are based on wishful thinking rather than historical fact. The roots of Freemasonry are in the medieval stonemasons' guilds that were infiltrated by men of learning in the seventeenth century. The initial secrecy of the guilds had more to do with guarding the tricks of the trade than lost wisdom. Alternative historians can always fall back on the idea that the knowledge in question was so powerful it had to be hidden behind secret symbolism to keep it out of the wrong hands, a claim that's hard to disprove but not especially convincing.

See also: Freemasonry; The Illuminati, the Alumbrados and the Templars; Noetic Science; The Rosicrucians; Paine, Thomas; Pike, Albert.

Ancient Mystery Schools

In *The Lost Symbol*, Langdon uses the term "Ancient Mysteries" to refer to the powerful lost wisdom of the ages. Rather confusingly, the term can also be used to describe some of the ancient cults and societies mentioned in the novel.

The terms "Mysteries" and "Mystery Schools" are used to refer to the secret religious cults of the ancient world, which are regarded by some as the forerunners of societies such as the Freemasons.

The religion of the ancient Egyptians was steeped in ritual, and many secret initiations developed. Some historians have claimed that the first ever secular secret societies grew out of Egyptian religious cults. For example, the "Brotherhood of Imhotep" was a secret society that worshipped the Egyptian poet, astronomer, physician and builder as a man rather than a god. Their worship of his building skills has led some esoteric researchers to draw parallels between the Brotherhood of Imhotep and the Freemasons.

In Greece, secret societies developed from mystery religions such as the Eleusinian Mysteries, which Robert Langdon refers to in Chapter 24 of *The Lost Symbol*. The Eleusinian Mysteries celebrated the myth of Demeter, the goddess of grain and fertility in Greek mythology. Secret rites and ceremonies of initiation, said to unite the worshippers with the ancient deities, were held in the city of Eleusis, near Athens.

Secret religions were hugely popular in ancient Rome, with hundreds of cults to deities such as Mithras, Isis and Bacchus. Some, like the Mithras cult, even had different ranks through which a candidate could pass, similar to the degree system of modern Freemasonry. In Chapter 20 of *The Lost Symbol*, Robert Langdon explains the influence of one of these cults, the Vestal Virgins, on the architecture of the U.S. Capitol Building. Langdon connects the rotunda of the Capitol Building with the Temple of Vesta, where a secret order of female priests guarded a sacred eternal flame, which the Romans believed was tied to the fortunes of their city.

As discussed in the sections "Ancient Mysteries" and "Pyramids and Ancient Egypt," there's a long tradition of writing that traces Freemasonry back to these secret religions and fraternities, from the eighteenth-century French author Jean Terrasson's influential novel *Sethos* to the writing of Manly P. Hall in the early twentieth century. But such writings are invariably based on intriguing analogies between Freemasonry and the ancient groups, rather than genuine historical connections.

In the chapter "Freemasonry and the Ancient Mysteries" of his 1898 book *The History of Freemasonry*, the famous nineteenth-century Masonic scholar Albert Mackey concludes that such analogies are best explained by the human inclination to conceal spiritual truth:

> The Mysteries and Freemasonry were both secret societies, not necessarily because the one was the legitimate successor of the other, but because both were human institutions and because both partook of the same human tendency to conceal what was sacred from the unhallowed eyes and ears of the profane. In this way may be explained the analogy between the two institutions which arises from their secret character and their esoteric method of instruction.

See also: Ancient Mysteries; Pyramids and Ancient Egypt.

The Apotheosis of Washington

In Chapters 21 and 133 of *The Lost Symbol*, Robert Langdon examines *The Apotheosis of Washington*, a fresco in the rotunda of the Capitol Building. Dan Brown uses the fresco to introduce the idea of the divine possibilities of man, which he links to both ancient knowledge and Noetic Science.

The Apotheosis of Washington is a large fresco by the Italian artist Constantino Brumidi that was painted over the course of eleven months at the end of the Civil War, shortly after a new dome was built on the Capitol Building to replace the original wooden one.

Brumidi was born in Rome in 1805 and demonstrated a talent for painting from an early age. He worked at the Vatican for Pope Gregory XVI and at the palace of Prince Torlonia before emigrating to the United States in 1852. As Robert Langdon suggests in Chapter 21, Brumidi spent much of his life working on the Capitol Building, where he was also responsible for the ornately decorated corridors on the first floor of the Senate Wing known as the "Brumidi corridors."

The Apotheosis of Washington is Brumidi's best-known work, and was completed in 1865. It depicts George Washington rising to heaven flanked by the goddess Liberty to his right and the goddess Victory to his left. Next to the two goddesses are thirteen maidens forming a circle, each holding a star to represent the thirteen original states.

It's thought that the fresco was inspired by the description of George Washington's death in *A History of the Life and Death, Virtues and Exploits of General George Washington* by Mason Locke Weems. This fanciful account of Washington's life is responsible for many popular myths, such as Washington's confession that he cut down his father's cherry tree with his hatchet, and his prayer at Valley Forge during the Revolutionary War. Weems's description of Washington's ascension to heaven is an example of the kind of writing you just don't get in political biography anymore:

> Swift on angel's wings the brightening saint ascended; while voices more than human were warbling through the happy regions, and hymning the great procession towards the gates of heaven. His glorious coming was seen afar off; and myriads of mighty angels hastened forth, with golden harps, to welcome the honored stranger.

In truth, Washington's death was a rather messier affair. As detailed in the section "George Washington," it's likely that he died as a result of the bloodletting he underwent to treat a cold. Although he asked for his body to be kept out of his coffin until three days after his death, this was probably because he was afraid of being buried alive rather than because he was expecting some angels to take him up to heaven. Nonetheless, the writing of Weems shows the exalted status of George Washington in the early nineteenth century, and Brumidi's fresco demonstrates that the hero worship was still raging in 1865.

Examining this depiction of George Washington becoming a god makes Robert Langdon reflect on apotheosis, the process of transformation from human to divine. The notion that an individual could be elevated to the status of a god was a common theme in ancient religion, from the belief in the divine lineage of Egyptian pharaohs to the worship of Roman emperors as gods by imperial cults. The idea that the divine aspect lies within man was also important to the ancient religious movements that have become known as Gnosticism, and features in the Gnostic Gospels.

Below George Washington, the goddesses and the maidens are six allegorical scenes, arranged to form a larger circle (which makes Robert Langdon see an echo of the circumpunct symbol in the fresco at the end of the book, although he's seeing them everywhere by this point).

A war scene shows the personification of Freedom with a sword, cape, helmet and shield that's also seen in Thomas Crawford's bronze statue on top of the Capitol's dome. Freedom is fighting tyrannical figures with the help of an eagle with arrows in its claws.

A scene representing science shows the Roman goddess Minerva alongside Benjamin Franklin, Samuel Morse and Robert Fulton.

In the scene representing marine achievements, the Roman sea god, Neptune, rides a chariot made from a shell, while the goddess Venus helps to lay some transatlantic telegraph cable.

A scene depicting commerce shows the Roman god Mercury giving a bag of gold to Robert Morris, the merchant known as the "Financer of the Revolution," for the money he gave to Washington's troops in the Revolutionary War.

A scene representing mechanics shows the god of fire, Vulcan, next to a cannon and a stack of cannonballs, with a steam engine in the background.

Finally, a scene representing agriculture shows the goddess Ceres sitting on the mechanical reaper designed by Cyrus McCormick, while the goddess Flora gathers flowers in the foreground.

Robert Langdon is fascinated by the juxtaposition of ancient divinity and scientific progress in these scenes. They suggest the idea that technology can bring miraculous, godlike powers to man, mirroring Katherine Solomon's belief that the pseudoscience of Noetics will unlock the divine potential of humanity.

See also: The Circumpunct; The United States Capitol; Washington, George.

Bacon, Francis

As Robert Langdon runs behind Washington, D.C.'s Folger Shakespeare Library in Chapter 73 of *The Lost Symbol*, he remembers that it houses the original Latin manuscript of Francis Bacon's *New Atlantis*. He claims that the book inspired the forefathers of America to found their new nation.

Sir Francis Bacon was an English philosopher and statesman, widely regarded as the most influential writer of the seventeenth century. Born in 1561, he attended Trinity College, Cambridge, from the age of twelve and entered Parliament at the age of twenty-three.

In 1620 he published *Novus Organum*, which sets out a series of procedures for isolating the cause of a phenomenon. These procedures became known as the Baconian Method, and were an important forerunner of the scientific method. According to John Aubrey's *Brief Lives*, Bacon was so committed to the experimental method that he became a martyr to it, dying from pneumonia he caught while testing to see if snow could preserve meat.

In 1627, a year after his death, Bacon's incomplete utopian tract *The New Atlantis* was published. The novel depicts a mythical land, Bensalem, where science and religion coexist in complete balance. Within this perfect land is a college called Solomon's House, where scientific experiments are conducted to advance society.

Many have linked Bacon to the Rosicrucians, the secret society that was allegedly formed in medieval Germany, and was the subject of much writing in the early seventeenth century. Although Rosicrucianism isn't mentioned in *The New Atlantis*, historians such as Frances Yates have argued that the book was heavily influenced by the movement. Certainly, it's easy to see Solomon's House as a Rosicrucian fraternity where intellectuals collaborate for the benefit of mankind. Some people, including Dean Galloway in Chapter 85 of *The Lost Symbol*, have gone as far as to speculate that Bacon might have even founded the Rosicrucians under the pseudonym of Christian Rosenkreuz. Although to be fair to Dean Galloway, he's just about to admit that there's no evidence for this when Robert Langdon interrupts him.

Whether they were actually written by the same person or not, *The New Atlantis* and the Rosicrucian Manifestos both chimed with the mood of utopianism in mid-seventeenth-century England, and probably helped to inspire the formation of the Invisible College and the Royal Society (although Bacon is not thought to have been a member of the Invisible College itself, as Robert Langdon suggests in Chapter 30).

To those who believe that America was founded as a "Masonic republic," it was this sense of utopian possibility that inspired the Freemasons of the early eighteenth century to estab-lish the United States. They argue that, influenced by Bacon and Rosicrucianism, the Masons created a real-life Utopia across the Atlantic. But as noted in the "Masonic Republic" section, the truth is slightly more complicated. Although Freemasonry was no doubt a huge influence on the Founding Fathers, they weren't all members of the fraternity, and there were plenty of Masons on both sides in the Revolutionary War.

See also: The Invisible College; Masonic Republic; The Rosicrucians; Utopia.

The Circumpunct

In Chapter 86 of *The Lost Symbol*, Robert Langdon places his hand in the stone box that contained the capstone of the Masonic pyramid. Pressing his finger down, he finds the indentation of a circumpunct on it. This symbol—a circle with a dot in the middle—has great significance to the novel, and Brown uses it to tie several of his themes together.

Perhaps unsurprisingly for such a simple symbol, the circumpunct has many different meanings. As Robert Langdon notes, it had important spiritual meaning in ancient Egyptian religion, Eastern philosophy, the Kabbalah and to the followers of Pythagoras. It's been associated with the sun since Egyptian hieroglyphics and ancient Chinese script. As gold was associated with the sun in alchemy, it also became the symbol for gold.

In Freemasonry, the symbol is known as "the point within a circle" and has much symbolic meaning. It's connected with the Supreme Being in Masonic writing, as in this passage from

Morals and Dogma, Albert Pike's tome outlining the degrees of the Scottish Rite:

> The creative energy of the deity is represented as a point, and that point in the center of the Circle of immensity. It is to us in this degree, the symbol of that unmanifested Deity, the Absolute, who has no name.

A common explanation of the symbol is that the point represents the individual Mason, and the circle is the boundary line of his duty to God and man. Sometimes an open book is drawn above the circle to represent "the Volume of Sacred Law," which is the book on the altar of a Masonic lodge. Although this book is often the King James Bible, it's important in Freemasonry to use terms that are inclusive of all faiths, such as "The Great Architect of the Universe." With the Volume of Sacred Law at the top, the point within a circle represents the importance of sacred texts in maintaining a balance in life.

The point within a circle also appears with two parallel vertical lines on either side of it in Freemasonry, which represent St. John the Baptist and St. John the Evangelist. Many interpretations have been given for this. For example, it's sometimes suggested that, because the feast days of John the Baptist and John the Evangelist are separated by six months, the symbol shows the path of the earth around the sun, with the lines representing the summer and winter solstices.

Dan Brown uses the different meanings of the circumpunct to tie several of his themes together in *The Lost Symbol*. It is associated with the wisdom of the ancients, with divinity and with the gold of alchemists. Peter Solomon exploits these connections to pretend to Mal'akh that the circumpunct is the "lost word" of the ancients that will enable him to complete his own alchemical transformation from man to god.

See also: Freemasonry; The Great Architect of the Universe.

Deism

In Chapter 111 of *The Lost Symbol*, Robert Langdon remembers attending a lecture at the Phillips Exeter Academy (the school Dan Brown attended). In the lecture, Peter Solomon discusses the religious beliefs of America's Founding Fathers. When a pupil suggests that America was founded as a Christian nation, Solomon tells him that in fact the country's forefathers were deists.

Deism is the belief that a supreme being created the universe, and that the existence of such a being can be proved through reason and observation of nature. Deists usually reject the possibility of divine intervention in human affairs through events such as miracles and revelations, and regard holy books as human works of interpretation rather than the word of God. Deists are often confused with atheists, who don't believe in any kind of god, as is famously exemplified by

Theodore Roosevelt's dismissal of Thomas Paine as a "dirty little atheist."

Deism gained popularity among intellectuals and freethinkers in the seventeenth and eighteenth centuries as scientific knowledge expanded. The work of Galileo, Kepler and Copernicus disproved the notion that the earth was the center of the universe, and called into question the scientific authority of the Bible. Furthermore, Isaac Newton's experiments suggested a world that adhered to precise mathematical laws, which increased skepticism about supernatural events such as miracles. These breakthroughs popularized the analogy of God as a cosmic clockmaker who designed the universe and set the laws of nature in motion, but did not intervene in its running.

Although many Americans would share the assumption that their country was founded as a Christian nation, Peter Solomon is to some extent right to claim that its founders were deists. But his assertion is something of a generalization: the question of which Founding Fathers were full-on deists and which simply had a liberal attitude toward Christianity is still contested.

There's not much controversy in the case of Thomas Paine. He published the famous three-part work *The Age of Reason*, which passionately advocated deism and criticized Christianity, bringing to the deist cause the same rhetorical skill that he'd brought to the struggle for independence in *Common Sense*. Paine stood firm in his beliefs despite the hostile reaction that his work often provoked.

Benjamin Franklin made explicit reference to his deistic beliefs in his autobiography and even published a pamphlet rejecting Christian dogma. Thomas Jefferson also demonstrated strong deistic tendencies, and at one point he even created his own personal Bible, the "Jefferson Bible" (mentioned in Chapter 131 of *The Lost Symbol*), stripping away all references to supernatural events such as miracles.

The case for George Washington holding such beliefs is rather weaker, however. It is often inferred that he was a deist from his failure to mention Christianity in his writings and his apparent refusal to take Communion. But, though it would make the case for the deism of the Founding Fathers much stronger, there is no direct evidence that Washington was a deist.

Accounts of the beliefs of the Founding Fathers are sometimes muddled by the misconception that deism is closely tied to Freemasonry. But as Robert Langdon's lecture in Chapter 6 of *The Lost Symbol* points out, Freemasonry was intended to be a haven from religious divisions. The term "The Great Architect of the Universe" was intended as an all-inclusive description of a supreme being, a term that would not exclude any particular religious belief. Deism was no more endorsed in the lodges than any other specific religious creed. Many instances of both Freemasonry and deism can be found in the Founding Fathers, but this might simply be because both were popular in the late-eighteenth century.

Nonetheless, many Americans would be surprised to find how widespread both deism and Freemasonry were at the time their country was founded. It certainly leaves the desire of the religious right to "return the country to the Christian principles on which it was founded" on shaky ground.

See also: Franklin, Benjamin; Freemasonry; The Great Architect of the Universe; Jefferson, Thomas; Paine, Thomas; Washington, George.

Dürer, Albrecht

When Katherine Solomon reads "1514 A.D." on the box of the Masonic pyramid's capstone, she assumes it's a date. Robert Langdon, however, realizes that the letters "A.D." are the initials of the German artist Albrecht Dürer.

Albrecht Dürer is regarded as one of the greatest of all German artists. Born in Nuremberg in 1471, he was the son of a goldsmith, and the godson of the most successful publisher in Germany, Anton Koberger. After serving an apprenticeship to the painter and printmaker Michael Wolgemut, Dürer opened his own workshop in 1495 and, in the years until his death in 1528, he produced many woodcut prints, copper engravings, watercolors and oil paintings, as well as theoretical writing on subjects such as measurement and human proportion.

Dürer's best-known works include the series of woodcuts known as *The Apocalypse* and the engravings *Knight, Death and the Devil*, *St. Jerome in His Study* and *Melencolia I*. The last of these is the engraving that Robert Langdon is reluctant to view online when the original is in a nearby gallery, partly because he's an art connoisseur, and partly because he knows how much less dramatic that would look in the inevitable Ron Howard movie.

Melencolia I depicts the winged personification of Melancholy, sitting with her head in her hand and looking dejected, surrounded by objects, including a dog, an hourglass, a bell and the tools of carpentry. Given the number of cryptic symbols that are packed into it, it's no wonder that hundreds of different interpretations have been given to the print. In accordance with the wider themes of *The Lost Symbol*, Langdon sees the engraving as symbolic of man's struggle to understand the Ancient Mysteries and achieve apotheosis, the transformation from the human to the divine.

It's significant that Brown used Dürer's works as a clue to solving the message on the Masonic pyramid, as some have claimed Dürer was an early Mason, even though he died almost two centuries before the establishment of the Grand Lodge of England in 1717. These claims are based on the apparent Masonic symbolism in his work, such as the compasses, hourglass, smoothly finished stone sphere and pair of scales in *Melencolia I*.

Several other works by Dürer have been cited as evidence that he was an early Mason, such as his woodcut for the title page of Messahalah's *De Scientia Motus Orbis*, which shows an astronomer holding a pair of compasses and a globe. However, rather than take this as evidence that Dürer was a Mason, and therefore that speculative Freemasons secretly existed in sixteenth-century Germany, it should be noted that compasses were already established as a symbol of creation in

Christian art. The Austrian National Library has, for example, an illustrated Bible dating from the early thirteenth century that shows God as an architect shaping the world with a set of compasses.

Another aspect of *Melencolia I* that fascinated Brown is the magic square that can be seen underneath the bell in the top right corner. As Langdon notes, the rows, columns, diagonals, center squares, corner squares and the four quadrants all add up to thirty-four (I bet Dan Brown wishes they added up to thirty-three; *see* Thirty-three). The magic square is then used as a transposition cipher to turn the letters on the Masonic pyramid into "Jeova Sanctus Unus" (Latin; loosely, "one true god").

The same transposition cipher can be used to turn the tiny 4 x 4 grid of letters on the dust jacket of the U.S. edition of *The Lost Symbol* into the phrase "Your Mind is the Key." This phrase certainly seems to echo *The Lost Symbol*'s theme of Noetic Science, but if the tradition of Dan Brown's cover clues is to be followed, it could also hint at the subject matter of Robert Langdon's next adventure (*see* Kryptos; The Widow's Son).

See also: Ancient Mysteries; *The Apotheosis of Washington*; Freemasonry; Magic Squares.

Franklin, Benjamin

In *The Da Vinci Code*, Robert Langdon fails to realize that the words "a pope" refer not to a leader of the Catholic Church, but to the eighteenth-century English poet Alexander Pope. He makes a similar mistake in *The Lost Symbol*, when he initially fails to understand that "The Order Eight Franklin Square" on the Masonic pyramid refers not to an address but to an order-eight magic square published by Benjamin Franklin in 1769.

Benjamin Franklin was a notable polymath, achieving success as an author, printer, statesman, politician, mathematician, scientist and inventor. He was also the only Founding Father who was a signatory on all three foundation documents of the United States: the Declaration of Independence, the Treaty of Paris and the Constitution.

Born in 1706, he was the fifteenth child of Josiah Franklin, a soap and candle maker. His father could afford to send him to school for only two years, so Franklin had to rely on self-education once his schooling ended when he was ten. He rose rapidly in the printing trade, and by 1730 he had taken over the *Pennsylvania Gazette*.

Franklin made his mark in a number of remarkably disparate fields. He sold tens of thousands of books, writing the annual *Poor Richard's Almanac* series under the pseudonym Richard Saunders. In Chapter 106, Mal'akh refers to the series as evidence of Franklin's interest in astrology. While the almanacs certainly contained astrological information, they were pretty wide-ranging, and also contained proverbs, aphorisms and poems.

Franklin is regarded as one of the greatest scientists of the eighteenth century for his discoveries relating to electricity. As a diplomat, he was responsible for bringing France in on the side of the colonies in the Revolutionary War. He was also a prodigious inventor, creating the lightning rod, bifocal glasses and even the flexible urinary catheter.

As Robert Langdon recalls in Chapter 6 of *The Lost Symbol*, Franklin was also a Freemason, and it's for this reason that he's sometimes drawn into the theory that the U.S. was founded as a "Masonic Republic." In 1730, he published the first documented evidence referring to Freemasonry in America with an exposé of Masonic rituals in the *Pennsylvania Gazette*. Franklin became a Mason himself the following year, joining Philadelphia's St. John's Lodge. He was elected as Junior Grand Warden in 1732, and became Grand Master in Pennsylvania in 1734.

As a publisher, Franklin was in a unique position to promote Masonry in America. In 1734, he published Reverend John Anderson's *Constitutions*, the book that had attempted to standardize the rituals and practices of Freemasonry in London.

Franklin kept up his keen interest in Masonry when he traveled to Europe. In 1760, he was received at the Grand Lodge of England in London's Crown and Anchor tavern. As mentioned in Chapter 30 of *The Lost Symbol*, Franklin was also inducted into the Royal Society, where Langdon suggests he might have been privy to secret ancient wisdom.

In 1778, while working as a diplomat in France, he joined the influential Loge des Neuf Soeurs (Lodge of the Nine Sisters, a reference to the nine Muses), and assisted the initiation of the French philosopher Voltaire into the lodge. Also in France, he joined the Loge de Saint-Jean de Jérusalem and the Loge des Bons Amis.

As Peter Solomon points out in Chapter 131, Franklin had unorthodox religious beliefs. Franklin mentions in his autobiography that he was at one point a deist, and he's often drawn into accounts of how deism was the "secret religion" of the Founding Fathers.

Franklin died in 1790, at the age of eighty-four. His funeral was attended by more than twenty thousand people, but surprisingly he was not buried with Masonic honors. This is because his original lodge was not recognized by contemporary ones in Pennsylvania, due to a schism between "ancient" and "modern" Masons. It was the kind of trivial conflict between divisions of Masons that renders especially ludicrous the theories about the fraternity as a unified force who want to take over the world.

As with George Washington, it's easy to see how Franklin

was influenced by the values of Freemasonry. Like Washington, he had little formal education, but was dedicated to the self-education and self-improvement central to Freemasonry. Also like Washington, Franklin believed in the Masonic value of tolerance to all religious creeds that Robert Langdon discusses in Chapter 6.

See also: Ancient Mysteries; Deism; Freemasonry; The Invisible College; Masonic Republic; Paine, Thomas.

Freemasonry

It's long been known that Dan Brown's third Robert Langdon novel would involve the Freemasons. Shortly after the release of *The Da Vinci Code*, Brown's own website referred to this in the "Frequently Asked Questions" section. Explaining why he had such an interest in secret societies, Brown mentioned that he grew up in New England, "surrounded by the Masonic lodges of our Founding Fathers." He ended the section by letting the following slip: "The next Robert Langdon novel . . . is set deep within the oldest fraternity in history . . . the enigmatic brotherhood of the Masons."

It comes as no surprise that Langdon and the Masons should bump into one another eventually. Brown made prominent use of the secret societies the Illuminati and the Priory of Sion in the first two Langdon novels. The Freemasons are the most famous secret society of all, even if, as Robert Langdon himself acknowledges in Chapter 6 of *The Lost Symbol*, they're not really that secret (although for the sake of Brown's thriller they're a "society with secrets").

Many Freemasons worried that *The Lost Symbol* would cast them as the bad guys, especially as Langdon claimed in Chapter 11 of *Angels and Demons* that they had been infiltrated by the Illuminati. However, when *The Lost Symbol* came out it was clear that Dan Brown admired the fraternity's religious tolerance, and chose to depict them in a positive light, even if he couldn't resist adding macabre details like the human skull in the Prologue.

As the name suggests, Freemasonry has its origins in the building craft. In the Middle Ages, stonemasons used knowledge of geometry to build huge structures such as cathedrals. They kept this knowledge secret by organizing themselves into guilds. As well as keeping the tricks of the trade under wraps, these guilds would ensure that new craftsmen were apprenticed. This would typically involve a seven-year apprenticeship to reach the level of Fellow Craft, and many further years of experience to reach the status of Master Mason, at which point the apprentice would learn the handshakes and passwords that would identify him to other members of the fraternity.

Many of the rules of behavior for early Masons were described in a document known as *The Regius Manuscript*, which has been dated to around 1390. Entitled *A Poem of Moral Duties*, this 794-line work lays out the moral conduct expected of Masons, such as honesty and reliability, and traces the mythical history of Masonry back to ancient Egypt.

It's not clear exactly why Masons became known as the Freemasons. One theory is that the term is a shortened form of "free stone masons," who were skilled workmen who shaped softer rock known as free stone. Another theory is that free masons were those who were not tied to regular employment, and could travel from one place of employment to another.

The advent of the printing press in the sixteenth century meant it became harder for Masons to guard their secrets. The financial value of the craft of masonry declined, but the fraternity was still admired, especially for its moral values. Masonic lodges started to accept members who hadn't been instructed in the craft, and Freemasonry began its transformation from an elevated trade union to a philosophical fraternity.

By the mid-seventeenth century, it was necessary to differentiate between operative Freemasons (those who knew what to do with a chisel) and speculative Freemasons (those who were attracted to the principles of the fraternity, but wouldn't be much use if you needed a flying buttress knocking up). The Masonic quest for self-betterment appealed to the kind of utopian thinkers who were forming the Invisible College and the Royal Society, and the ranks of speculative Freemasons grew.

This gentrification of Freemasonry continued throughout the seventeenth century, and in 1717 the Grand Lodge of England was formed. Six years later, the Reverend James Anderson published the first edition of *The Book of Constitutions*. This book, which was greatly influenced by *The Regius Manuscript*, aimed to standardize the rituals of Freemasonry among the London lodges that made up the Grand Lodge.

The Book of Constitutions introduced a theological element that would become key to Freemasonry. Instead of pledging belief in a Christian God, Freemasons would now name only a supreme being known as "The Great Architect of the Universe." As discussed in the section on the Great Architect of the Universe, the vagueness of this term has allowed anti-Masonic theorists to claim that all Masons are secret deists, or even that the Great Architect of the Universe is really Satan. However, the truth is that religious discussion was forbidden in lodges, and the name was adopted as a nonspecific term for a supreme being to respect individual religious belief.

Freemasonry went global as the British Empire expanded in the eighteenth century. The Grand Lodge awarded an official charter to St. John's Grand Lodge, Boston, in 1733, although there were many unrecognized lodges already in existence by then. Benjamin Franklin published the first Masonic book in America in 1734, a reprint of *The Book of Constitutions*. Freemasonry clearly played a role in the Revolutionary War and the founding of America, although exactly how much of a role it played is hotly disputed. This is one of the themes of *The Lost Symbol*, and is discussed in the "Masonic Republic" section of this book.

In the early nineteenth century, Freemasonry was shaken by the mysterious disappearance of a businessman from New York named William Morgan. In 1825, Morgan attempted to join a Masonic lodge in Batavia, a town in upstate New York. He was rejected, and intended to vent his frustration by writing a book called *Illustrations of Masonry by One of the Fraternity*, which would expose their secret rituals. Soon afterward, Morgan went missing, and there are conflicting accounts of what happened to him. A group of local Masons claimed that they'd paid him to emigrate to Canada, but many at the time believed Morgan had been the victim of a Masonic ritual murder and that his body had been dumped in the Niagara River.

Six men were tried in court for Morgan's murder, but they were acquitted. When it emerged that the judge, prosecutor and most of the jury were Freemasons, there was a public outcry. The case became a national scandal, and Freemasonry was hit hard. Membership plummeted by 60 percent over the next decade, and some lodges were forced to close. A single-issue political party named the "Anti-Masonic Party" was formed in 1828, which took almost 10 percent of the vote in the presidential election in 1832.

By the end of the nineteenth century, Freemasonry in America was getting back on track. Albert Pike's reworking of the Scottish Rite had popular appeal, and membership began to rise again. But Freemasonry was still tainted for many by the Morgan affair. The idea that anyone who gives away the mysteries of the fraternity will be murdered was established in the public imagination, and still survives to this day, even though thousands of books and websites detailing the "secrets" of the Masons are available.

The most recent golden age for Freemasonry was the 1950s, when the fraternity's ranks swelled to more than five million in the United States alone. It became less fashionable in the 1960s, as, to the baby-boomer generation, it smacked too much of the establishment. Since then, there's been a steady decline in membership numbers, but there are still thought to be more than five million Masons worldwide. This is a pretty impressive number, even if it is dwarfed by the cult of Dan Brown. The publication of *The Lost Symbol* has done much to bring the Masons back into the spotlight, and it will be interesting to see if lodges manage to exploit this and boost their membership.

Thanks to its supposed secrecy, Freemasonry has inspired an inordinate number of fantastical conspiracy theories, such as the ones Mal'akh recalls watching a TV documentary about in Chapter 57.

Yet, although it's still widely regarded as a secret society, it's not difficult to find out the rituals, passwords and symbols of Freemasonry, as so many exposés have been published. One of the major plot strands in *The Lost Symbol* involves Mal'akh attempting to release a secretly filmed video of a Masonic ceremony that includes Supreme Court judges, prominent senators, the Secretary of Defense and the director of the CIA. Although such a video would no doubt get a decent number of hits on YouTube, it's pretty implausible that it would bring down the government and inspire a witch hunt. Rather than appearing sinister and threatening to the outside world, most Masonic ceremonies would just look a bit silly.

Many Masonic theories insist that, instead of a quaint society of retirees, the Freemasons are a cabal of Machiavellian schemers intent on nothing less than world domination. For such people, the Masons are a "modern Illuminati" who function at the highest levels of society, waiting for their moment to overthrow civilization as we know it and establish a New World Order. But if you turn up at your local lodge expecting to join this sinister cabal, you are likely to be disappointed.

From the fabrication that the Masons are powerful, shadowy plotters come theories involving them in every unsolved mystery and fantastical conspiracy imaginable. Countless books, websites, pamphlets and letters written in green ink have claimed that the Masons assassinated John F. Kennedy, engage in Devil worship, faked the Apollo moon landings and carried out the September 11th attacks. Lodges were even banned in Germany in 1935, as Hitler was convinced that Jews and Freemasons were secretly working together in order to achieve world domination. Which should give you all the encouragement you need to resist turning into an anti-Masonic conspiracy buff.

These outlandish Masonic theories were famously spoofed in an episode of *The Simpsons* where Homer tries to join the local "Stonecutters' Lodge." In this episode, the fraternity reveal the sinister truth in a song, proclaiming:

Who leaves Atlantis off the maps?
Who keeps the Martians under wraps?
We do! We do!

The lyrics go on to detail a series of ever more absurd conspiracy theories.

The only accusation aimed at Freemasonry by its detractors that has some basis in truth is that it encourages cronyism. Although Freemasons take an oath against favoring fellow Masons over nonmembers, many instances of corruption have been uncovered in organizations such as the British police. Sadly for conspiracy fanboys, these scandals are pretty humdrum compared to the other stuff they imagine Masons getting up to. They might not be filming moon landings in the Nevada desert or assassinating presidents, but they are being promoted to chief inspector ahead of their peers.

In contrast to these anti-Masonic theories, some alternative accounts of the history of the fraternity portray them as heroic guardians of powerful wisdom. Authors like Manly P. Hall have argued that Masonry is descended from the Mystery Schools of Egypt, the Kabbalists of Judaism and ancient alchemists. These ideas feature prominently in *The Lost Symbol*, with both Peter Solomon and Robert Langdon describing the legend that the Freemasons are the guardians of secret lost wisdom known as the "Ancient Mysteries." In truth, Freemasonry has its roots in medieval stonemasons' guilds rather than pre-Christian mystics, but Brown exploits the myth satisfyingly to serve his plot and his New Age ideas about human potential.

Many Freemasons will be breathing a sigh of relief that Brown chose to depict them as a benevolent organization guarding ancient wisdom rather than a shady villainous cabal, although it could have worked out in their favor even if he hadn't. Maybe being the bad guys would have made them sexy enough to attract an influx of young new members.

Dan Brown's sympathetic portrayal of the fraternity disappointed many conspiracy buffs, who have countered by drawing Brown himself into their theories. For them, Brown was poised to expand upon the account of Freemasonry as a front for the Illuminati that he gave in *Angels and Demons*, but as he carried out his research he realized he'd go the same way as William Morgan if he revealed the truth, so he chickened out and made them the heroes. This seems like unfounded nonsense to me. But then again, that's exactly what I'd have to say, isn't it?

See also: The Great Architect of the Universe; The Illuminati, the Alumbrados and the Templars; The Invisible College; Pike, Albert; The Scottish Rite; Solomon's Temple.

The George Washington
Masonic National Memorial

In Chapter 76 of *The Lost Symbol*, Robert Langdon makes the CIA think he's heading for the George Washington Masonic National Memorial by asking Omar the cabdriver the direction of Alexandria, Virginia. Agent Simpkins then waits for Langdon and Katherine Solomon at the memorial while they make their way to Washington National Cathedral instead.

The George Washington Masonic National Memorial is situated on the top of Shuter's Hill, the highest point in Alexandria, and the site of a Union fort during the Civil War. The cornerstone was laid in 1923, and the building was completed in 1932, funded entirely by contributions from Freemasons. The building is 333 feet tall, and was inspired by the Pharos or lighthouse of Alexandria, which, like the Great Pyramids at Giza and the Statue of Zeus at Olympia that inspired Horatio Greenough's Washington statue, was one of the Seven Wonders of the Ancient World.

The memorial houses a museum containing many of George

Washington's Masonic artifacts, such as his apron, sash, tools and the trowel he used to lay the cornerstone of the United States Capitol. It contains many notable depictions of Washington, such as murals by Allyn Cox showing him at the Capitol cornerstone ceremony and at a Masonic service in Philadelphia in 1778 to mark the evacuation of the British Army. At the end of the building's Memorial Hall, there's a statue of Washington in full Masonic regalia designed by Bryant Baker.

The Alexandria Lodge Number 22, which Washington belonged to, meet regularly in the building, and have constructed a replica of the eighteenth-century lodge room that Washington used to attend. On the top floor there's an exhibit representing the throne room of Solomon's Temple, sponsored by a Masonic appendant body called the "Tall Cedars of Lebanon." Elsewhere, there are various exhibits sponsored by other appendant bodies, such as a display on the charitable work of the Ancient Arabic Order of Nobles of the Mystic Shrine.

Although it gets only a cameo role in *The Lost Symbol*, the memorial was featured alongside the House of the Temple, the Smithsonian Museum Support Center and the U.S. Botanic Garden as one of the locations for the novel on NBC's *The Today Show*.

See also: Freemasonry; Pyramids and Ancient Egypt; The Shriners; Solomon's Temple; The United States Capitol; Washington, George; Washington Zeus.

The Great Architect of the Universe

In Chapter 6 of *The Lost Symbol*, Robert Langdon speaks positively about the religious tolerance and open-minded attitudes of the Freemasons. He says that to keep the fraternity open to men of all different faiths, they use the general term "The Great Architect of the Universe" (also known as the Grand Architect of the Universe).

The Great Architect of the Universe, sometimes abbreviated to GAOTU, is the term used to refer to the Supreme Being in Masonic ceremonies. It can be traced back to James Anderson, a Scottish preacher living in early eighteenth-century London. Anderson was appointed to combine all the existing Masonic documents into an instructional manual that would be distributed to lodges. The result, entitled *The Constitutions of the Free-Masons*, was published in 1723.

Anderson introduced the nonspecific term because Free-masonry was intended as a haven from the religious bickering of the outside world. Discussion of religious issues was to be forbidden in Masonic lodges, and Anderson adopted the allegorical name, which was already established in the writings of Thomas Aquinas and John Calvin, as a nonsectarian reference to a supreme being.

While Freemasonry assumes a belief in God, it encourages religious freedom and respects the privacy of personal belief. The society promotes a series of morals and values, but it regards these as compatible with all religions. The term "Great Architect of the Universe" was adopted so that members of separate faiths could concentrate on the Supreme Being and not their religious differences.

The vagueness of the term is sometimes exploited to reveal the supposed "true purpose" of the fraternity by anti-Masonic theorists. More than a century after Léo Taxil admitted that his exposés of Satanic Freemasons were a hoax you'll still find fundamentalist Christian books and websites claiming that "The Great Architect of the Universe" worshipped by Masons is in fact Satan. One such site even makes the staggeringly unconvincing claim that this must be so because GAOTU is almost an anagram of "goat."

See also: Deism; Freemasonry; Satanism.

The Great Seal of the United States

In Chapter 30 of *The Lost Symbol*, Langdon claims that the legend of a Masonic pyramid in Washington, D.C., stems from the pyramid on the Great Seal of the United States.

Regular Dan Brown readers will be familiar with the Great Seal, as Robert Langdon explains its symbolism to Vittoria Vetra in *Angels and Demons*. He tells her that noticing the symbolism on the dollar bill was the thing that first sparked his interest in the Illuminati. He also refers to the eye inside the pyramid as the "trinacria" and explains that the symbol, familiar from Masonic lodges around the world, stands for the ability of the Illuminati to watch all things.

Langdon certainly wasn't the first to read hidden meanings into the symbols of the Great Seal. Indeed, they've inspired decades of frenzied speculation, and have been used to accuse the U.S. government of everything from Masonic infiltration to Satanism.

The front of the Great Seal shows an eagle holding an olive branch in one claw, and a bundle of arrows in the other. Above the eagle's head thirteen stars are arranged to form a hexagram, a reference to the union of the original thirteen colonies that formed the United States. This has led some conspiracy theorists into an anti-Semitic fantasy in which the stars are said to form a Star of David, which is taken as evidence of a Jewish conspiracy in the U.S. government. In its beak, the eagle holds a banner reading "E pluribus unum," meaning "Out of many, one."

This Latin motto also appears in Constantino Brumidi's *The Apotheosis of Washington*, which is featured in *The Lost Symbol*. As Langdon stares at the painting in the final chapter of the novel, he sees in the phrase an intriguing echo of the idea that divinity can emerge from the minds of mankind.

On the reverse of the Great Seal, we find the pyramid that Langdon suggests inspired the myth of a Masonic pyramid in Washington, D.C. Like the one Langdon finds in the U.S. Capitol, the pyramid is missing its capstone. In Chapter 39 of *The Lost Symbol*, Langdon suggests that the symbol of an unfinished pyramid appears on the Great Seal as a reminder that the U.S. has not yet achieved its potential, and there's work to be done. While this certainly fits in well with the novel's theme of man's divine potential, it should be remembered that the Great Pyramid at Giza, which probably inspired the image, is also missing its capstone. At the bottom of the pyramid, the year 1776 is written in Roman numerals. This obviously refers to the date of the Declaration of Independence in the

United States, although this hasn't stopped some conspiracy buffs claiming that it actually refers to the year that Adam Weishaupt founded the Order of the Bavarian Illuminati.

At the top of the pyramid is a depiction of an eye inside a triangle, which is known as the All-Seeing Eye. This is sometimes interpreted as proof that the Freemasons were infiltrated by the Illuminati, as Robert Langdon details in *Angels and Demons*. In accordance with the wider themes of the new novel, however, Langdon gives a far broader account of the All-Seeing Eye in *The Lost Symbol*. He now suggests that the origin of the All-Seeing Eye is the circumpunct, a symbol associated with the Ancient Mysteries.

Two Latin mottoes appear on the seal. Above the pyramid and the eye is written "Annuit coeptis," which is translated as "He has favored our undertaking," i.e. God has favored the American cause. Underneath the pyramid is a motto reading "Novus ordo seclorum." This is generally translated as "A new order of the ages," an announcement of the new American era. However, to many conspiracy theorists, and indeed to Robert Langdon in *Angels and Demons*, the word "seclorum" is translated not as "of the ages" but as the modern word "secular," meaning nonreligious. This mistranslation is then said to contradict the first motto, and betray the true beliefs of the Founding Fathers. Some journey even further from accurate translation and claim the phrase means "New world order," the ultimate goal of the Illuminati.

There are two further theories relating to the Great Seal that turn up in *The Lost Symbol*. In Chapter 35, Langdon notes that there are thirteen storage rooms beneath the Capitol, and is reminded of the theory about the recurrence of the number 13 on the Great Seal. On the reverse of the seal, the pyramid has thirteen steps and there are thirteen letters in the phrase "Annuit coeptis." On the front of the seal, there are thirteen letters in the phrase "E pluribus unum," thirteen stars above the eagle, thirteen leaves on the olive branch, thirteen arrows in the eagle's talons and thirteen bars on the shield in front of the eagle.

Some conspiracy buffs have linked this recurring number to the thirteen degrees of Templar initiation as a sign that the U.S. government was infiltrated by the Knights Templar posing as the Freemasons. Others have linked it to the number of witches that make up a coven to suggest the Satanic inclinations of the Founding Fathers. Others have sensibly remembered that thirteen was in fact the number of colonies that joined to form the United States. (Incidentally, both "The Lost Symbol" and novel's original title "The Solomon Key" have thirteen letters. Just throwing it out there, conspiracy fans.)

In Chapter 75 of *The Lost Symbol*, Katherine Solomon exploits another famous Great Seal theory to create a red herring. She superimposes the Seal of Solomon over the Great Seal with the All-Seeing Eye at the top point. Doing this highlights the letters "A" and "s" from "Annuit coeptis" and "N," "o" and "m" from "Novus ordo seclorum," producing an anagram of the word "mason." Langdon and Solomon pretend that this is a clue pointing them to the George Washington Masonic National Memorial in Alexandria, Virginia, while they actually travel to Washington National Cathedral.

The real story of the seal's origins is pretty mundane in

comparison to the conspiracy theories. The design of the seal was overseen by Charles Thomson, the secretary of Congress, in 1782. Congress had appointed three committees to come up with a design, but had failed to find one they were happy with, showing a remarkable lack of cohesion for a cabal bent on world domination. Thomson incorporated elements generated by all three committees, and managed to get a design accepted. Unfortunately for conspiracy buffs, there's no evidence that Thomson was even a Freemason, let alone a member of the Illuminati plotting a New World Order.

Thomson intended the pyramid to stand for the strength and durability of the new nation, and it seems understandable that you'd choose something surviving from the ancient world to announce that you'd be around for a long time. The Eye of Providence and the motto "He has favored our undertaking" were a reference to the belief that God had aided the United States in the Revolutionary War.

But even if we accept that the design of the Great Seal wasn't devised as a sign of Masonic infiltration, it can still be argued that the decision to place it on the dollar bill was. The Great Seal first appeared on the back of the dollar bill in 1935. The idea of putting it there is attributed to Henry A. Wallace, who was the Secretary of Agriculture in President Franklin D. Roosevelt's cabinet. He was apparently drawn to the motto "A new order of the ages," which he associated with Roosevelt's New Deal. But as several people, including Robert Langdon in *Angels and Demons*, have pointed out, Wallace and Roosevelt were both Freemasons at a time when the Eye of Providence was established as a Masonic symbol. Whether you take this as proof that Wallace and Roosevelt were secret Illuminati members is a different matter.

Looking into the facts around the Great Seal might not provide much evidence for the outlandish theories it's attracted. But it's little surprise that the Seal continues to hold a fascination for Dan Brown, who loves to reveal the hidden symbolic meanings of images we see every day.

See also: The Apotheosis of Washington; The Circumpunct; Freemasonry; The Illuminati, the Alumbrados and the Templars.

Hall, Manly P.

The Lost Symbol begins and ends with quotations from the esoteric author Manly P. Hall's book *The Secret Teachings of All Ages*. The novel begins with the quotation "To live in the world without becoming aware of the meaning of the world is like wandering about in a great library without touching any of the books," and in the final chapter, Robert Langdon recalls a sentence from the conclusion of Hall's book: "If the infinite had not desired man to become wise, he would not have bestowed upon him the faculty of knowing."

The influence of Manly P. Hall can be seen throughout *The Lost Symbol*, and Brown's conception of such things as the Hand of the Mysteries and the Ancient Mysteries seems to have been shaped by Hall.

Manly Palmer Hall was born in Peterborough, Ontario, Canada, in 1901 and moved to Los Angeles, California, at the age of eighteen. He published the landmark book *The Secret Teachings of All Ages* in 1928, when he was just twenty-seven. Rather than researching a specific field, Hall had decided to study the whole subject of esotericism, covering, as the full title of the book states, "Masonic, Hermetic, Qabbalistic and Rosicrucian Symbolical Philosophy" to show how ancient civilizations had mystical powers that are lost to modern man. It was a huge tome, measuring 13 inches by 19 inches and weighing more than 14 pounds, but even so Hall managed to sell out an initial run of more than 1,000 copies at $100 each. The success of the book inspired a genre of writing about modern society's hidden roots, and transformed Hall into a sagelike figure.

Using funds from some of the acolytes he had attracted, Hall founded the Philosophical Research Society in 1934 near Griffith Park in Los Angeles. This included the Philosophical Research Library, which contains more than 50,000 books and was envisaged by Hall as a modern equivalent of the Ancient Library of Alexandria. The library was used by Carl Jung to research his 1944 book *Psychology and Alchemy* and was regarded as so important by President Franklin D. Roosevelt that he came up with plans to safeguard its contents after the bombing of Pearl Harbor in 1941.

Hall applied his esoteric knowledge to patriotic purpose in the war, constructing an elaborate theory about how the continent of America had been marked as the site of a philosophic empire by ancient Egyptians, which he aired in his book *The Secret Destiny of America*. He claimed that mystical Egyptian orders had charged the site with spiritual and emotional forces and that Plato's writings about Atlantis were a veiled reference to it.

Hall doesn't provide much solid evidence for his mystical theories. He wasn't interested in unearthing facts about ancient civilizations and early religion in the way that a modern archaeologist or anthropologist might be, but in drawing connections between ancient texts to reveal the "universal wisdom" in them. Nonetheless, Hall sparked an interest in a vast array of philosophical and religious traditions, and his work continues to influence esoteric and New Age writing, as well as authors of fiction such as Dan Brown.

Hall remained immensely prolific throughout his life, writing more than fifty books and delivering more than 8,000 lectures before his death in 1990, covering subjects such as pagan rites, Greek philosophy, Eastern religions and Freemasonry. He was awarded the thirty-third degree of the Scottish Rite in 1973 for his speculation about the ancient roots of the fraternity.

See also: Ancient Mysteries; The Hand of the Mysteries; Mal'akh; Pyramids and Ancient Egypt.

The Hand of the Mysteries

In Chapter 13 of *The Lost Symbol*, Robert Langdon realizes that Peter Solomon's severed hand has been tattooed to resemble "the Hand of the Mysteries," an ancient summons to an initiate to receive secret knowledge.

Dan Brown's account of the Hand of the Mysteries was influenced by Manly P. Hall's book *The Secret Teachings of All Ages*. In it, Hall details how a hand covered in symbols was an invitation to enter the temple of wisdom, and replicates an engraving of a decorated hand from *L'Antiquité expliquée et représentée en figures*, an eighteenth-century book by the Benedictine monk Bernard de Montfaucon.

One of the color plates in Hall's book is of a painting of the Hand of the Mysteries by J. Augustus Knapp. It shows an outstretched palm with a key, lantern, sun and star on the fingers and a crown on the thumb. In a passage underneath the illustration, Hall claims that it represents the hand of a Master Mason, and that the individual symbols have specific meaning:

The key represents the Mysteries themselves, without whose aid man cannot unlock the numerous chambers of his own being. The lantern is human knowledge, for it is a spark of the Universal Fire captured in a man-made vessel . . .

The sun, which may be termed the "light of the world" represents the luminescence of creation through which man may learn the mystery of all creatures which express through form and number.

The star is the Universal Light which reveals cosmic and celestial verities. The crown is Absolute Light—unknown and unrevealed—whose power shines through all the lesser lights.

Hall compares the image to religious hand-painting, such as a print showing the twelve Apostles on the phalanges of the fingers, and the figure of Christ and the Virgin Mary on the thumb. He suggests that the hand is a common symbol of divinity, as in images of the hand of God emerging from a cloud. There are certainly many religions in which the hand has symbolic meaning, such as the Hand of Fatima in Islam, which stands for the five fundamentals of faith, prayer, pilgrimage, fasting and charity, and the hand that symbolizes the vow of Ahimsa in Jainism (see Appendix). In Hinduism and Buddhism, hundreds of symbolic hand gestures known as mudras are used in religious ritual.

The severed hand of Peter Solomon also recalls the "hand of glory," a magical charm used in the sixteenth century. This was a candle made from the severed hand of a hanged convict that had been embalmed in oils and herbs. It was said to render anyone who came across it motionless, and was popular with thieves, who believed it gave them the power to enter houses undisturbed.

See also: Ancient Mysteries; Hall, Manly P.

The House of the Temple

The House of the Temple in Washington, D.C., is the setting for both the Prologue and the climax of *The Lost Symbol*. Situated at 1733 Sixteenth Street NW, it's the headquarters of the Southern Jurisdiction of the Scottish Rite, an appendant body of Freemasonry.

Completed in 1915, the temple was designed by John Russell Pope, the architect who was also responsible for the Jefferson Memorial (and who could be the subject of the message encrypted on the back of *The Lost Symbol*, "Popes Pantheon"— *see* Widow's Son). Surprisingly, Pope wasn't in the fraternity himself, but he collaborated with thirty-second-degree Mason Elliott Woods, who oversaw the building's symbolism.

The building is rife with Egyptian symbols that have been adopted by the Masons, such as the Sphinx, the Ankh and the Uraeus. A huge pyramid sits on top of the temple, which David Ovason links to the unfinished pyramid on the U.S. dollar bill in his book *The Secret Architecture of Our Nation's Capital* as a suggestion of covert Masonic power in U.S. government. In *The Lost Symbol*, this connection is exploited as part of Mal'akh's secret film of the Masons. Standing in front of the House of the Temple, he shoots a close-up of the Great Seal's pyramid as it appears on the one-dollar bill. He then pulls the dollar away to reveal the House of the Temple's pyramid.

Inside the temple there's a case displaying the Masonic Lodge flag that Buzz Aldrin took to the moon with him. Or rather, if we're in the realm of conspiracy theory here, the flag that Buzz Aldrin took to the Nevada desert with him when he pretended to go to the moon.

There's also the Hall of Honor that Robert Langdon walks down in Chapter 125. As he passes through the corridor, Langdon notices an oil painting of Harry S. Truman, the thirty-third president of the United States (surprisingly, he doesn't drag this into his theory about the number 33). Other notable Masons honored in the hall include Gene Autry, the performer who was famous as "the singing cowboy" in the 1930s and 1940s, World War II hero Jimmy Doolittle, and Norman Vincent Peale, author of the self-help bestseller *The Power of Positive Thinking*.

The Temple contains the remains of Albert Pike, the Freemason who rewrote the Scottish Rite and served as the Sovereign Grand Commander of the Scottish Rite's Southern Jurisdiction for more than thirty years. It contains the bronze bust of Pike that Langdon notices in Chapter 121, along with the inscription of his famous quotation, "What we have done for ourselves alone dies with us; what we have done for others and the world remains and is immortal."

On September 11, 2009, NBC's *The Today Show* ran a segment about the House of the Temple as part of its series on the locations of *The Lost Symbol*, suggesting that many Washington commuters drive past the building every day without realizing its significance. As with the London and Paris locations featured in *The Da Vinci Code*, and the Rome locations of *Angels and Demons*, the House of the Temple is now likely to get a new influx of visitors.

See also: Pike, Albert; Washington, D.C.

The Illuminati, the Alumbrados and the Templars

In Chapter 30 of *The Lost Symbol*, Robert Langdon suggests that stories about powerful wisdom being protected by secret organizations such as the Templars, the Illuminati and the Alumbrados all have their roots in the Ancient Mysteries. He suggests that throughout history secret brotherhoods have formed to prevent the knowledge of the ancients falling into the wrong hands, and the Freemasons were the last of these groups to survive.

Of the three groups, the Alumbrados is the one that will be least familiar to regular Dan Brown readers, although they've been referred to once before in the Langdon series. In Chapter 63 of *Angels and Demons*, Gunther Glick and Chinita Macri mention the theory that the Illuminati can be traced back to the Alumbrados. While it's true to say that the word translates as "illuminated," there's no historical link between this mystical sixteenth-century Spanish group and the Illuminati of eighteenth-century Bavaria. The Alumbrados, however, did believe in the possibility of the human mind becoming divine, and were persecuted by the Spanish Inquisition for their un-orthodox beliefs, so they fit well into Langdon's account of history's secret groups.

Dan Brown readers will remember the Illuminati from *Angels and Demons*. Although that novel's depiction of them as a group surviving to this day was fiction, they were a real fraternity at one point, founded by the university law professor Adam Weishaupt in eighteenth-century Bavaria. In 1776, Weishaupt formed a secret society he called the "Order of the Perfectibilists," because they believed that human nature could be perfected through constant self-improvement. As the organization grew in size, it became better known as the "Illuminati." Weishaupt was a freethinker who opposed the Catholic Church and believed that corrupt governments around the world should be replaced with a global authority—the notorious New World Order that crops up in so many paranoid fantasies.

It's certainly true that Weishaupt had connections with the Masons, though he was more interested in exploiting their success than passing on the wisdom of the ancients to them. In Freemasonry, he found a framework in which he could incorporate his own ideas about the re-education of mankind. Higher Illuminati degrees were devised to follow on from the three basic degrees of Freemasonry, enticing many existing Masons to join Weishaupt's society.

As Freemasonry grew in popularity, the Illuminati spread with it, thanks to Weishaupt's crafty manipulation. But his success was short-lived. In 1784, the Bavarian Elector banned all secret societies, including both the Illuminati and the Freemasons. Worried that he would be arrested for treason, Weishaupt fled Bavaria for Gotha. With Weishaupt in exile, the society soon died out, although it lived on in the imagination of conspiracy theorists. The Illuminati have since become a catch-all name for alternative historians, the shadowy cabal you can fall back on when you need to connect the dots in your conspiracy theory. Almost all the major world events of the last couple of centuries have been attributed to them, from the American Revolution to the Holocaust to the September 11th attacks. In fact, conspiracy theorist and former *BBC Breakfast Time* presenter David Icke reckons they're reptiles from the constellation Draco who live in caverns underneath the earth. If that ever turns out to be the final twist in a Dan Brown novel, I'll be going right back to the bookshop to get my money back.

However, the one thing you can't claim about the Illuminati is that they were guardians of ancient knowledge. All the evidence suggests that Weishaupt's Illuminati kept anything relating to mysticism, esotericism and alchemy out of their rituals.

The Templars will also be familiar to Dan Brown fans, as they were featured in *The Da Vinci Code*, where they were explicitly linked to the Freemasons. In Rosslyn Chapel, Langdon explains to Sophie Neveu that the Masons and the Knights Templar have strong historical ties.

Founded in 1118, the Knights Templar were an army of warrior monks who escorted bands of pilgrims to Jerusalem

he Crusades. They set up headquarters inside the al-
ısque on Mount Moriah, the former site of King
Solomon's Temple.

The Knights Templar were initially known as the Poor
Knights of Christ, as they relied on donations to survive, but
they soon accumulated vast wealth. Officially endorsed by the
Catholic Church in 1129, they received donations of money
and land from those keen to help the fight in the Holy Land,
and were allowed to keep what they looted from Muslims.
Pilgrims journeying to the Holy Land began to place their assets
in the hands of the knights, who would safeguard them for a fee,
making them a very early form of international bank.

When Islamic forces regained control of Jerusalem in 1239,
the order was forced to resettle in Cyprus and France. But with
their military purpose less significant, support for the Knights
declined. On Friday, October 13, 1307 (a date which is incor-
rectly said to have inspired the Friday the 13th superstition),
many members of the order were arrested by the misleadingly
named King Philip the Fair of France. They were charged with
heresies such as worshipping Baphomet, an idol with a goat's
head, and were tortured to extract false confessions. The
Grand Master of the order, Jacques de Molay, was burned at
the stake in Paris in 1314.

While there are certainly intriguing links between these
mysterious persecuted groups, it would be difficult to draw any
of them into a narrative about how the secret knowledge
of the ancients was passed down to the Freemasons. As mentioned, Adam Weishaupt's Illuminati were certainly linked to
the Masons, but they were not concerned with hidden ancient

knowledge. The Alumbrados had been wiped out by the Spanish Inquisition long before speculative Freemasonry. The Knights Templar had also disappeared well before the foundation of the United Grand Lodge of England in 1717, although some alternative historians have claimed otherwise. For example, Richard Leigh and Michael Baigent (two of the authors of *Holy Blood, Holy Grail* who tried to sue Dan Brown for plagiarism in 2005) claim in their 1989 book *The Temple and the Lodge* that some Knights Templar escaped the purge of the early fourteenth century and that the order eventually developed into Freemasonry. For them, the Knights found refuge in Scotland, where they helped the Scots fight the English for independence. They then joined forces with local stonemasons' guilds and founded speculative Freemasonry. In this alternative history, the order existed in this secret form until the eighteenth century.

They claim that evidence of this transitory stage can be found in the Templar-Masonic symbolism of Rosslyn Chapel in Midlothian, such as the carving in the southwest corner of the chapel that seems to show a Knight Templar participating in a Masonic ritual. However, others have claimed that this was merely an elaborate take on Christian iconography, probably referencing the biblical passage, "Let them alone: they be blind leaders of the blind. And if the blind lead the blind, both shall fall into the ditch" (Matthew 15:12–14). They also point out that the only link between the Knights Templar and Sir William St. Clair, who founded the chapel in the mid-fifteenth century, was that members of the St. Clair family testified *against* members of the Knights Templar who were brought to trial in Edinburgh in 1309. So it's unlikely that the Knights Templar would ever have gotten the chance to pass on secret ancient knowledge to the Masons.

The notion that secret fraternities throughout history have communicated powerful ancient knowledge to the Freemasons certainly makes for an intriguing exercise in alternative history, but it fails to convince when you look into the facts about secret brotherhoods.

See also: Freemasonry; The Rosicrucians.

The Invisible College

In Chapter 30 of *The Lost Symbol*, Robert Langdon suggests that secret wisdom originating in the Mystery Schools of Egypt ended up in the hands of the Invisible College in London.

The Invisible College was a group of scientists including Robert Boyle, Robert Hooke, John Wilkins and Christopher Wren who held regular meetings in England in the mid-seventeenth century.

The college was "invisible" because it was an informal network of intellectuals exchanging ideas rather than a physical building, although the mysterious overtones of the name have made the group attractive to alternative historians.

The chemist and physicist Robert Boyle (of Boyle's Law fame) makes several references to an "invisible" or "philosophical" college in letters written in 1647 and 1648. The group held informal meetings at Gresham College in London, and following the restoration of Charles II in 1660, they formed a "Colledge for the Promoting of Physico-Mathematicall Experimentall Learning." Two years later, Charles II approved an official charter for the group, which became known as the Royal Society.

The Royal Society crops up frequently in anti-Masonic theory. While it shouldn't be surprising that a society that has existed for nearly 350 years should have contained a few Masons, you could make a case that the fraternity had a strong presence in the early days. Several inaugural members such as Robert Moray, Christopher Wren, Elias Ashmole and William Stukeley are known to have been Masons, while many of the society's other notable early figures, including Robert Boyle and Isaac Newton, have also been linked to Freemasonry.

Members of the Invisible College and the Royal Society were brought together by a desire to attain knowledge through experimental methods, and were influenced by Francis Bacon, whose works had helped to establish the scientific method. The notion that a group of preeminent intellectuals should share ideas and knowledge could also have been influenced by the utopian strain in Bacon's works, such as *The New Atlantis*, which imagines a remote society governed by a group of elders.

As Robert Langdon notes, Masonic Founding Father Benjamin Franklin is known to have visited the Royal Society on his visit to London in 1757. He might simply have wished to talk science with some of the finest minds of his generation. But in the imaginations of pseudo-historians, he was discussing his plot to establish a Masonic Republic in the New World or learning the secret lost wisdom of the ancients. Langdon is also right to claim that many notable modern scientists such as Stephen Hawking are members of the Royal Society, although the moniker "Invisible College" is long gone.

While it's certainly true that over the last three and a half centuries the Royal Society has had several members, such as Sir Isaac Newton, who were interested in ancient knowledge, I'm sure the scientists who comprise the group today would be surprised to learn that they're the guardians of the lost knowledge of the Egyptian Mystery Schools.

See also: Bacon, Francis; Utopia.

Jefferson, Thomas

In Chapter 131 of *The Lost Symbol*, when Peter Solomon is telling Robert Langdon that the Ancient Mysteries were passed down through history in the Bible, he mentions that Thomas Jefferson created his own version of the Bible to extract its hidden meaning.

Thomas Jefferson, the third president of the United States and the primary author of the Declaration of Independence, was born in Virginia in 1743, the third of eight children. His father died when he was fourteen, leading him to inherit more than 5,000 acres of land and dozens of slaves. Jefferson graduated from the College of William and Mary in Williamsburg with the highest honors in 1762, and went on to achieve success as a statesman, architect, archaeologist and inventor, among other things.

It is known that Jefferson attended meetings at the Loge des Neuf Soeurs (Lodge of the Nine Sisters) in Paris with Benjamin Franklin and that a lodge in Virginia was named

"Jefferson Lodge" in 1801, but there's no evidence that he was ever actually a Freemason. This is a shame for alternative historians, as it would certainly strengthen theories that the United States was founded as a "Masonic Republic" if they could find a record of him joining a fraternity.

Jefferson can be much more successfully drawn into theories about the unconventional religious attitudes of the Founding Fathers, however. Peter Solomon is right that Jefferson created his own personal version of the Bible, although it would be a stretch to claim he did this to extract secret ancient wisdom.

The "Jefferson Bible," which he named *The Life and Morals of Jesus of Nazareth*, arranges extracts from the Gospels of Matthew, Mark, Luke and John into chronological order, creating a single narrative, and removes references to supernatural events to focus on the ethical teachings of Christ. Accordingly, it ends on a bit of a downer, with Jesus being crucified but not resurrecting.

To understand why he did this, it's important to understand the popularity of deism at the time of the Founding Fathers. Deists believe that a supreme being created the universe, and that the existence of this being can be proved through reason. They also deny the possibility of divine intervention through such things as miracles. It's easy to see how the influence of this belief would have inspired Jefferson to strip away the supernatural references in the Christ story but preserve its moral teachings. It might also explain the deistic overtones of some of the terms Jefferson used in the Declaration of Independence, such as "Nature's God."

Jefferson died on July 4, 1826, fifty years after the adoption of the Declaration of Independence, and was buried on his estate in Charlottesville, Virginia.

See also: Deism; Masonic Republic; Paine, Thomas.

Kryptos

Longtime fans of the Robert Langdon series will no doubt have been waiting for the sculpture *Kryptos* to turn up in *The Lost Symbol*, but Brown teasingly leaves this until near the end of the novel. It's long been anticipated that the sculpture would make an appearance, and an unofficial guide to Dan Brown's books has even been published with a picture of it on the front. Although alert fans will have realized that the document containing the words "It's buried out there somewhere" that's alluded to at the very start of the book is the solution to *Kryptos*, the sculpture itself doesn't make an appearance until Chapter 127.

Kryptos is a sculpture by the artist James Sanborn, located in the courtyard outside the headquarters of the Central Intelligence Agency in Langley, Virginia. The sculpture, dedicated in November 1990, contains four separate encrypted messages that have brought it to the attention of cryptography enthusiasts. Nearly twenty years later, the fourth of these messages remains undeciphered, rendering it one of the most famous unsolved puzzles in the world.

The work is technically made up of several sculptures, the large S-shaped wave of copper inscribed with text being the best-known part of it. This part of the sculpture was brought to the attention of Dan Brown fans when the map reference 37° 57' 6.5" North and 77° 8' 44" West was written backward on the cover of the U.S. edition of *The Da Vinci Code*. The "Uncover the Code Challenge" section of Dan Brown's official website featured the question "What enigmatic sculpture stands one degree north of the location indicated in the code?" Adding on this extra degree leads to *Kryptos*.

The sculpture's inscription contains four messages, each encrypted with a different cipher. Although the first three have been cracked, the fourth remains unsolved, and it's thought that the sculpture will present an additional puzzle once all the individual sections have been decoded. This fourth section, which is referred to as K4, contains ninety-seven characters and has been called "the Everest of codes." Thousands of people, from the CIA's own professional cryptographers to amateur code crackers, have scrutinized it, but so far to no avail.

As well as the map reference, a further clue pointing to *Kryptos* can be found on the U.S. jacket of *The Da Vinci Code*. If you look closely at the rip effect on the back of the dust jacket, you can make out the phrase "Only WW knows" written upside down underneath the quote from Vince Flynn. This is a reference to the decoded second part of *Kryptos*, which includes the words "Who knows the exact location? Only WW." In an interview with *Wired* magazine, James

Sanborn confirmed that the "WW" in question was William H. Webster, who was director of the CIA between 1987 and 1991. However, Sanborn denied that he gave Webster the complete solution to *Kryptos* in a sealed envelope, claiming that he merely misled the CIA into believing they had the whole solution. So while it might well be a "fact" that a document containing cryptic text is locked in a CIA safe, as Dan Brown claims at the start of *The Lost Symbol*, this document might not give all the answers required. At any rate, the impenetrable secrecy surrounding the fourth section of *Kryptos* renders it an apt, if somewhat subversive, sculpture for the intelligence agency of the U.S. government.

In *The Lost Symbol*, Nola Kaye and Rick Parrish realize that a seemingly mysterious redacted document was actually the CIA employee discussion forum about the sculpture. Looking at the various pieces of the work, they recognize that it's a code made of different pieces, or *symbolon*, just like the Masonic pyramid, and wonder if *Kryptos* itself might contain some ancient Masonic secret.

Which probably won't come as great news to James Sanborn, who was deeply annoyed at the prospect of the sculpture featuring in a Dan Brown novel, according to the *Wired* magazine article.

See also: The Widow's Son.

Langdon, Robert

Robert Langdon is the protagonist of Dan Brown's bestselling novels *Angels and Demons, The Da Vinci Code* and *The Lost Symbol*. According to his website robertlangdon.com, he's a professor of "Religious Symbology" at Harvard University in Cambridge, Massachusetts, whose areas of research include "classical iconology, symbols of pre-Christian culture, goddess art and the decryption of ancient ciphers." While "symbology" is a fictitious academic field, an art history or theology professor might specialize in religious iconography (although they probably don't do so while solving clues in a touristy location accompanied by a beautiful woman who's just lost a close relative).

On his website, Langdon claims to have published more than a dozen books, including *The Symbology of Secret Sects, The Art of the Illuminati, The Lost Language of Ideograms* and a textbook entitled *Religious Iconography.*

Langdon has presumably been too busy saving the world from tattooed villains to update his site, as it lists *Symbols of the*

Lost Sacred Feminine as upcoming, yet we know from the comments of Pam from passenger services in the first chapter of *The Lost Symbol* that the book has already been released, and was the source of much controversy.

In Chapter 44, we find that Langdon's editor is called Jonas Faukman, and that Langdon has been late in submitting his new manuscript, presumably the follow-up to *Symbols of the Lost Sacred Feminine*. The name Jonas Faukman is an anagram of Jason Kaufman, Dan Brown's editor, who presumably made similar comments during the long wait for a sequel to *The Da Vinci Code*.

Some have detected a note of wish-fulfilment in the character of Robert Langdon, whose "uniform" of loafers, tweeds and turtleneck sweaters is suspiciously similar to the kind of outfit Dan Brown wears in author photos. Let's just hope that we never find out Langdon had a previous career as a singer-songwriter like Brown did. For most of the novel, Brown thankfully resists turning Robert Langdon's fame into an analogy for his own reluctant celebrity, although I'm going to hazard a guess that he got the idea for the first chapter, in which Langdon is greeted by a fawning fan before stepping into a limo with a basket of hot muffins inside, on a publicity tour.

In the witness statement that he gave to the High Court in London on December 21, 2005, Dan Brown described Robert Langdon as "an amalgam of many people I admire." One of these was a friend of Brown's father called John Langdon, who is a professor of typography at Drexel University. John Langdon created the famous ambigrams of the words "fire," "air," "water," "earth" and "illuminati" for *Angels and Demons*.

According to Brown's statement, another person who inspired the character of Langdon was Joseph Campbell, the writer and lecturer on mythology whose book *The Hero with a Thousand Faces* was a major influence on George Lucas when he created *Star Wars*. Brown apparently watched a TV show called *The Power of Myth*, in which Campbell discussed the deeper meanings of symbols, and aimed to imbue Langdon with the same "open-minded tone."

The influence of Joseph Campbell on Langdon is evident in Chapter 30 of *The Lost Symbol*, when Langdon remembers teaching students about "archetypal hybrids." Langdon traces the iconic element of good versus evil in myths, fairy tales and *Star Wars* in a way that recalls Campbell's theories about the journey of the archetypal hero in *The Hero with a Thousand Faces*.

Although the opening chapter of *The Da Vinci Code* describes Langdon as "Harrison Ford in tweed," Tom Hanks was cast in the role for Ron Howard's films of the novels. Hanks does a solid job of bringing the character to life, although the flowing mullet he sports in *The Da Vinci Code* is rather distracting. You'd think a symbologist of Langdon's caliber would be aware that styling your hair short on top and long at the back is a universally accepted symbol that you're a douche.

See also: Mal'akh; Solomon, Katherine.

Magic Squares

In Chapter 70 of *The Lost Symbol*, Robert Langdon examines the magic square in Albrecht Dürer's famous engraving *Melencolia I*. Later in the novel, an order-eight magic square published in 1769 by Benjamin Franklin turns out to be the key to decoding the mysterious symbols on the base of the Masonic pyramid.

In a magic square, numbers are arranged so that the sum of all the rows, all the columns and both the diagonals is the same. In an interview with the show *All Things Considered* on National Public Radio following the release of *The Lost Symbol*, Dan Brown revealed that he was introduced to magic squares at a young age by his father, a math professor and text-book author.

It's apt that Brown should include magic squares in the trail of clues to lost ancient wisdom, as they can be traced back to antiquity. The Chinese legend of Lo Shu, dating from around 650 B.C., features a turtle with marks on its back that represent the numbers from 1 to 9. The numbers are arranged in such a way that each row, column and diagonal gives the sum of 15. This became known as "The Lo Shu Magic Square."

4	9	2
3	5	7
8	I	6

The order of a magic square is the number of rows and columns it has, so the Lo Shu Magic Square would be called an order-three square. The Lo Shu Magic Square is also known as a normal square. A normal order-three magic square features all the numbers from 1 to 9, a normal order-four magic square features all the numbers from 1 to 16, and so on. The number that all the rows, columns and diagonals add up to is known as the magic constant. So in the Lo Shu Magic Square, the magic constant is 15.

Normal magic squares exist for all orders of number, except for the number 2. It's possible to construct an order-one magic square, but this would just be a square with the number one inside, and wouldn't impress anyone. As mathematicians regard magic squares as identical if you can obtain them by rotation or reflection, there is only one normal order-three magic square, which is the Lo Shu Magic Square. There are 880 normal magic squares of order four and 275,305,225 normal magic squares of order five. Nobody knows exactly how many normal order-six magic squares there are, but the number would probably look something like Dan Brown's bank balance.

The magic square that appears in Albrecht Dürer's engraving *Melencolia I*, which Robert Langdon uses to rearrange the letters given by the Masonic cipher, is a normal order-four magic square, with a magic constant of 34:

16	3	2	13
5	10	11	8
9	6	7	12
4	15	14	1

As Robert Langdon points out, it's not just the rows, columns and diagonals of this square that give the magic constant of 34 here, but also the four quadrants, the four center squares and the four corner squares.

The four quadrants give:

$$16 + 3 + 5 + 10 = 34$$
$$2 + 13 + 11 + 8 = 34$$

$$9 + 6 + 4 + 15 = 34$$
$$7 + 12 + 14 + 1 = 34$$

The four center squares give:

$$10 + 11 + 6 + 7 = 34$$

The four corner squares give:

$$16 + 13 + 4 + 1 = 34$$

In fact, the square's ingenuity doesn't stop there. Look at the two sets of four diagonally opposite numbers:

$$2 + 8 + 9 + 15 = 34$$
$$3 + 5 + 12 + 14 = 34$$

Look at the outer numbers that are one square along from the corners:

$$3 + 8 + 14 + 9 = 34$$

Look at the outer numbers that are two squares along from the corners:

$$2 + 12 + 15 + 5 = 34$$

And, finally, as Langdon points out, the two central numbers of the bottom row give the date of Dürer's engraving:

1514

Some Dan Brown fans with too much time on their hands have pointed out that the ISBN of *The Lost Symbol* (disregarding its "978" prefix) also adds up to Dürer's magic constant of 34:

$$0 + 3 + 8 + 5 + 5 + 0 + 4 + 2 + 2 + 5 = 34$$

It's pretty unlikely that this is deliberate, though. If Dan Brown had specially chosen an ISBN, I'm sure he'd have picked one that added up to 33, like the release date of the novel does $(9 + 15 + 0 + 9)$.

Robert Langdon uses Dürer's magic square as a transposition cipher to turn the letters "SOEUATUNCSASVUNJ" on the Masonic pyramid into "Jeova Sanctus Unus," the pseudonym of Isaac Newton. He mentions that Dürer's square was the first time a magic square appeared in European art and claims that this was an encoded way of showing that the lost secrets of the ancients were now being held by the secret societies of Europe.

Although Langdon doesn't flesh out this theory with details, he's right to claim that magic squares were once thought to have powerful mystical properties. For example, in Arabic culture, magic squares were used to protect disabled children, placed on the wombs of women in childbirth, and sewn into the shirts of soldiers. Islamic tradition places particular significance on squares with a magic constant of 66, as this corresponds to the numerical value of the word "Allah."

As Mal'akh recalls, the mystical powers of magic squares are revealed in Heinrich Cornelius Agrippa's famous study of occult philosophy *De Occulta Philosophia*, written in three books between 1509 and 1510. In it, he associates seven specific magic squares of the orders three to nine, which are sometimes called kameas, with each of the classical planets. In ceremonial magic, these kameas were used to construct the sigils, or magic symbols, of spirits. The letters of the spirit's name are converted into numbers, and the pattern that these numbers make on the kamea is used for the design of the sigil.

However, it's not a dusty grimoire that Mal'akh has to consult to find the magic square needed to solve the Masonic pyramid, but, rather disappointingly, his laptop. When he's trapped in the deprivation tank, Langdon realizes that the clue "The secret hides within the Order Eight Franklin Square" refers not to a mystical order located at Number 8 Franklin Square in Washington, D.C., but to an order-eight magic square devised by Benjamin Franklin. Mal'akh then dashes upstairs to look at Franklin's magic square on his laptop (he probably has it bookmarked right next to "Tattooed Homicidal Maniac's Forum").

In his autobiography, Benjamin Franklin describes being shown a book containing magic squares designed by the French mathematician Bernard Frénicle de Bessy. He says he first dismissed the squares as "incapable of any useful application," but admits that he's devised a number of them himself. Franklin went on to publish several magic squares, including the order-eight square that's reproduced in *The Lost Symbol*:

52	61	4	13	20	29	36	45
14	3	62	51	46	35	30	19
53	60	5	12	21	28	37	44
11	6	59	54	43	38	27	22
55	58	7	10	23	26	39	42
9	8	57	56	41	40	25	24
50	63	2	15	18	31	34	47
16	1	64	49	48	33	32	17

If you're especially good at mental arithmetic, or you're just the kind of person who keeps a calculator handy to check the mathematical claims made in thrillers, you'll notice that, despite what Mal'akh says, the diagonals on Franklin's square don't in fact add up to the same amount as the rows and columns, so this isn't a true magic square. But the sum of the rows and columns, 260, does occur in many intriguing patterns in the square. For example, look at the four corner squares and the four center squares:

$$52 + 45 + 16 + 17 + 54 + 43 + 10 + 23 = 260$$

When Franklin shared his order-eight square with a friend, he was shown the book *Arithmetica Integra* by the German mathematician Michael Stifel, which contained an order-sixteen square. That evening, Franklin went home and devised his own order-sixteen square, which also had many intriguing patterns (although he let himself down with the diagonals again). Franklin even experimented with the idea of magic circles, where numbers are arranged in concentric circles so that the sum of each circle and radius is identical.

Robert Langdon compares magic squares with another branch of recreational mathematics, Sudoku. Despite their resemblance to magic squares, Sudoku puzzles in fact developed from Latin squares, which are named after the Latin characters that the eighteenth-century Swiss mathematician Leonhard Euler used to demonstrate them. Latin squares are grids filled with numbers or symbols in such a way that none appear twice in the same row or column, as in the following example:

1	2	3
2	3	1
3	1	2

Sudoku puzzles use a 9 x 9 Latin square split into nine smaller 3 x 3 squares. To complete a Sudoku grid, you must fill it with the numbers 1 to 9 so that every number appears only once in every row, column and 3 x 3 square. Depending on the difficulty of the puzzle, some of the numbers are already filled in. Thanks to the Sudoku fad of the last few years, the Latin square is probably more common than the magic square today. But perhaps Dan Brown, with help from Albrecht Dürer and Benjamin Franklin, could help to draw our attention back to the magic square.

See also: Dürer, Albrecht; Franklin, Benjamin.

Mal'akh

Mal'akh is the tattooed villain of *The Lost Symbol*, who is introduced taking part in a Masonic ritual in the novel's Prologue. Previously called Andros Dareios and (SPOILER ALERT!!!) Zachary Solomon, Mal'akh changed his name in reference to the fallen angel Moloch from John Milton's *Paradise Lost*.

Mal'akh is covered in tattoos with mystical symbolism, some of which are important in Freemasonry. On his legs he has the pillars of Boaz and Jachin, which are the same pillars that Dan Brown used to link Rosslyn Chapel with Solomon's Temple and Freemasonry in *The Da Vinci Code*. These pillars, which are an important part of the Fellow Craft degree ceremony, are originally mentioned in the account of the building of Solomon's Temple in the Bible:

> Also he made before the house two pillars of thirty and five cubits high, and the chapiter that was on the top of each of them was five cubits.
>
> And he made chains, as in the oracle, and put them on the

heads of the pillars; and made an hundred pomegranates, and put them on the chains.

And he reared up the pillars before the temple, one on the right hand, and the other on the left; and called the name of that on the right hand Jachin, and the name of that on the left Boaz.

(2 CHRONICLES 3:15–17)

As Robert Langdon says in *The Da Vinci Code*, every Masonic lodge contains representations of these pillars. In Freemasonry, the pillars represent strength and establishment, and an initiate must pass through them on his way to Solomon's Temple as part of the second degree of Freemasonry, Fellow Craft. In Masonic lodges, the pillars have globes on top, which are said to represent the heavens and the earth, so it's possible that Mal'akh was attracted to the pillars as symbols of the transformation from human to divine that he wants to achieve.

On his chest, Mal'akh has a tattoo of a double-headed phoenix. This resembles the most famous symbol of Scottish Rite Freemasonry, the double-headed eagle. The double-headed eagle is a common symbol in heraldry, appearing on the coats of arms of the Roman Empire and the Byzantine Empire, as well as the flags of such countries as Serbia and Montenegro. In the Southern Masonic Jurisdiction of the Scottish Rite, it's always shown with its wings facing down. However, in the Northern Masonic Jurisdiction, an eagle with its wings pointing up is used to distinguish thirty-third-degree Masons.

The double-headed eagle has many symbolic meanings, but Dan Brown's use of it was probably influenced by Manly P. Hall's *The Secret Teachings of All Ages*. In the book, Hall associates the symbols of the double-headed eagle and phoenix with alchemy, and the process of human transformation that it represents:

> The double-headed eagle, or phoenix, subtly foreshadows the ultimate androgynous state of the human creature. Rosicrucian alchemy was not concerned with metals alone. Man's own body was the alchemical laboratory, and none could reach Rosicrucian adeptship until he had performed the supreme experiment of transmutation by changing the base metals of ignorance into the pure gold of wisdom and understanding.

This connection between the double-headed phoenix and inner rebirth is the reason the symbol attracted Mal'akh, who believes that by finding the lost word, he can unleash his divine power.

Tattoos are not the only way in which Mal'akh attempts his process of physical transformation. As Katherine Solomon sees when she looks at a series of photographs of him, he was obsessed with bodybuilding, and his excessive use of steroids changed his body shape and his facial features.

In Chapter 86, we find that Mal'akh is castrated, which he believes brings him closer to the state of androgynous wholeness that Manly P. Hall describes in the passage above. Mal'akh compares himself to Attis, the unfaithful lover of Cybele, who castrated himself when she drove him mad to get revenge. Followers of the cult of Cybele are thought to have castrated themselves in emulation of Attis. As Mal'akh suggests, there are still cults that encourage voluntary castration today, with a famous recent example being the UFO cult Heaven's Gate, whose followers committed mass suicide in 1997, to coincide with the appearance of the Hale-Bopp Comet.

Some reviewers have complained that Mal'akh is too similar to Francis Dolarhyde, the villain from Thomas Harris's thriller *Red Dragon*. Dolarhyde is also heavily tattooed and fascinated by the idea of transformation. He's obsessed with the William Blake watercolor *The Great Red Dragon and the Woman Clothed in Sun*, and believes that he can become the dragon by killing people. Interestingly, Moloch, the demon that Mal'akh named himself after, is also the subject of a famous Blake watercolor, *The Flight of Moloch*.

In Brown's defense, it's worth remembering that the connection between tattoos and transformation goes back much further than Thomas Harris. As Mal'akh notes in Chapter 2, tattoos have had symbolic meaning for thousands of years, and were important in ancient China, Egypt and India, as well as to European tribes such as the Celts and the Picts, so it's no surprise that a character seeking transformation would cover himself with tattoos.

See also: Freemasonry.

The Masonic Cipher

In Chapter 46 of *The Lost Symbol*, Langdon reveals that the symbols on the side of the Masonic pyramid are encoded with the Masonic cipher. He says that early Masons used this code to communicate with one another, but it's now been discarded, as it's too easy to break.

The Masonic cipher, which is also known as "the pigpen cipher," is a substitution cipher that replaces each letter of the alphabet with the symbol it appears next to on a grid such as the one below:

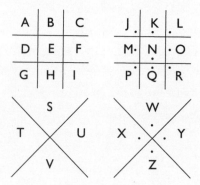

So following this grid, the words "The Lost Symbol" would be encrypted as:

THE LOST SYMBOL
>⊓⊏⊩⊏∨>∨<⊐⊔⊏⊩

The Masonic cipher is classed as a substitution cipher, as the units are in the correct order, but need to be altered. A very famous example of a substitution cipher is ROT13, which is an abbreviation of "Rotate by 13 places." To apply ROT13 to a piece of text, you simply have to replace each letter with the one thirteen places farther along in the alphabet, as shown below:

A B C D E F G H I J K L M
N O P Q R S T U V W X Y Z

So, using this code, "The Lost Symbol" becomes "Gur Ybfg Flzoby."

Given Dan Brown's love of codes, it was always a safe bet that his novel about the Freemasons would feature the Masonic cipher. The only question was how such a simple code could be made into a challenge for Robert Langdon. Brown gets around this by making the Masonic cipher only the first stage of encryption for the message on the pyramid. The text revealed by the Masonic cipher turns out be:

S O E U
A T U N
C S A S
V U N J

Decoding the next stage requires not another substitution cipher but a transposition cipher, which is one where the units are rearranged in a different order, but remain unchanged themselves. To solve this stage, they need to find the key used for the transposition cipher, which turns out to be the magic square in Albrecht Dürer's engraving *Melencolia I*.

See also: Dürer, Albrecht; Freemasonry; Magic Squares.

Masonic Presidents

In Chapter 125 of *The Lost Symbol*, Robert Langdon walks past the painting of President Truman in the Hall of Honor in the House of the Temple and tries to imagine him taking part in Masonic ceremonies.

Much anti-Masonic theory is concerned with the U.S. presidents who were members of the fraternity. It's sometimes said that the majority of U.S. presidents have been Masons, and that this is evidence of the Masonic desire to take over the world and establish a New World Order. Some paranoid theorists have even linked this to the recent wars in Iraq and Afghanistan, which they claim are the U.S.'s first step toward world takeover, even though George W. Bush was never a Mason (he was a member of the secret "Skull and Bones" society at Yale, but Brown is presumably saving this for another Langdon book).

Although conspiracy theorists have linked virtually every U.S. president with Freemasonry, only fourteen so far (out of the current forty-four) are known to have been members of the fraternity:

George Washington, 1st President, 1789–97
James Monroe, 5th President, 1817–25
Andrew Jackson, 7th President, 1829–37
James Knox Polk, 11th President, 1845–9
James Buchanan, 15th President, 1857–61
Andrew Johnson, 17th President, 1865–9
James Abram Garfield, 20th President, 1881
William McKinley, 25th President, 1897–1901
Theodore Roosevelt, 26th President, 1901–9
William Howard Taft, 27th President, 1909–13
Warren Gamaliel Harding, 29th President, 1921–3
Franklin Delano Roosevelt, 32nd President, 1933–45
Harry S. Truman, 33rd President, 1945–51
Gerald Rudolph Ford, 38th President, 1974–7

It's often stated that Thomas Jefferson was also a Mason, although no proof of this has ever been uncovered. It's also sometimes claimed that the thirty-sixth president, Lyndon Baines Johnson, was in the fraternity, but records at the Johnson City lodge in Texas show that he completed only the first Masonic degree, Entered Apprentice.

See also: Freemasonry; The House of the Temple; Jefferson, Thomas; Masonic Republic; Washington, George.

Masonic Republic

The role that the values and ethics of Freemasonry played in the founding of the United States is a key theme in *The Lost Symbol*, and several references are made to the nation's "Masonic forefathers."

Theories about Masonic forefathers are often classed as alternative or secret histories, although when you consider that George Washington laid the cornerstone of the Capitol Building wearing his Masonic apron, surrounded by members of local lodges and making traditional offerings of corn, wine and oil, it's hard to see what's so alternative or secret about them. It's a matter of historical fact that Freemasonry had an impact on the founding of the U.S. But would it be going too far to claim that the United States was intended to be a "Masonic Republic"?

Both Peter Solomon in Chapter 111 and Robert Langdon in Chapter 73 describe the founding of the U.S. as a utopian project. This is an important aspect of "Masonic Republic" accounts, which claim the forefathers of the U.S. aimed to establish a perfect society according to the values of Freemasonry. It's true that the utopian thought of the seventeenth century had an influence on the growth of speculative Freemasonry. Francis Bacon's *The New Atlantis* had described a land where reason and mysticism could coexist, and Rosicrucianism had popularized the idea of a secret brotherhood holding the mystical key to self-improvement. Progressive thinkers were drawn to the haven of societies like Freemasonry to discuss ideas that might be branded heretical by the Church. Such Masons would no doubt have been attracted to the idea of forging a new nation away from the stifling power of the Church and European monarchies. But it's a bit of a stretch to claim that Freemasonry was the driving force behind the Revolutionary War.

It's certainly true that there was a high percentage of Freemasons among America's Founding Fathers. George Washington was a dedicated Mason, and the first documented evidence of Freemasonry in America is found in a newspaper published by Benjamin Franklin, the *Pennsylvania Gazette*. Many of those who signed the Declaration of Independence were known Freemasons, including John Hancock, Robert Payne, William Hooper, Joseph Hewes, Richard Stockton, George Walton and William Whipple, and Masonic ties have been suggested for most of the other signatories at one point or another.

It's sometimes claimed that one of the most important landmarks on the road to the American Revolution, the Boston Tea Party, was a Masonic plot. On the night of December 16, 1773, a group of men dressed as Mohawk

Indians emerged from the Green Dragon Tavern, boarded three of the British East India Company's merchant ships and protested against a tax on tea by dumping more than 300 chests of it into Boston Harbor. While many of the protesters were members of the local St. Andrew's Lodge, the Green Dragon Tavern was also a meeting place for noted non-Masonic groups such as the Sons of Liberty and the North End Caucus, who were also involved in the protest.

Another famous incident in American history that crops up in theories about the Masonic foundation of the country is Paul Revere's "midnight ride" on horseback before the battles of Lexington and Concord. Revere, who was a Mason, was briefly detained by British troops, and in official accounts he managed to escape the following morning. However, in the alternative version of events, he gave a secret Masonic plea to British soldiers who were also in the fraternity, and was immediately released. Revere was then able to give the warning that helped to repel British troops. It certainly gives the famous tale an attractive twist for Masonic theorists. The idea that Masons are compelled to help one another by answering a secret plea that overrides all other loyalties crops up frequently in theories about everything from the secret impact of the fraternity on history to modern-day cronyism. But there's no evidence that Revere was really helped by his Masonic connections.

When considering the extent to which the U.S. began as a "Masonic Republic," it should be remembered that there were Masons on both sides of the conflict in the Revolutionary War, which is hardly surprising considering how popular the fraternity was in eighteenth-century Britain. Indeed, some of the first recorded instances of Freemasonry in America were the field ceremonies conducted by military lodges of the British Army.

While there's plenty of evidence that Freemasonry was important to many of the Founding Fathers, things get a bit less convincing when other secret societies are roped in. Thanks to its supposed secrecy, Freemasonry has been named as a front for everyone from the Illuminati to the Knights Templar, and alternative historians have exploited these spurious connections to devise elaborate theories about the early history of the U.S. We're told that the real reason the year 1776 is included on the Great Seal is because that was when Adam Weishaupt founded the Bavarian Illuminati, or that July 4 is celebrated because that was the date in 1187 when Muslim armies drove the Knights Templar from Jerusalem.

The Roman and Egyptian symbolism that Langdon notices in Washington, D.C., has inspired some theorists to claim that Masonic Founding Fathers were worshipping ancient gods while paying lip service to Christianity. Most ludicrously of all, Christian conspiracy theorists have claimed that the Masonic Founding Fathers were in fact Satanists who left behind them clues to their true beliefs such as the inverted pentagram above the White House on a street plan of Washington, D.C.

As membership of Freemasonry dwindles, it becomes easier to associate it with such claims. But to understand the role of the society in the founding of the U.S., it's important to consider what it meant in the eighteenth century. Freemasonry was a meeting place for intellectuals who were drawn to progressive thinking. It's no surprise that many of these freethinkers were also involved in efforts to cut colonial ties.

See also: Bacon, Francis; Franklin, Benjamin; The Great Seal of the United States; The Rosicrucians; Washington, George; Washington, D.C.

Newton, Isaac

In Chapter 30 of *The Lost Symbol*, it's mentioned that private papers belonging to Sir Isaac Newton, discovered in 1936, revealed his interest in alchemy and ancient wisdom. As regular Dan Brown readers will know, these aren't the first references to the great scientist in the Robert Langdon series. In *The Da Vinci Code*, one of the clues on the cryptex led Langdon and Sophie Neveu to Newton's tomb in Westminster Abbey.

Born in 1642 in Woolsthorpe, Lincolnshire, Isaac Newton was a physicist, mathematician, astronomer and alchemist and is regarded as one of the most influential scientists in history. The law of universal gravitation and the three laws of motion outlined in his book *Principia Mathematica* laid the foundation of classical mechanics and are among the most famous theories in the history of science.

In 1936, a collection of Newton's papers was auctioned at Sotheby's on behalf of the Earl of Portsmouth. The "Portsmouth Papers" included unpublished manuscripts relating to subjects that would now be classed as "occult." They showed that Newton was interested in alchemy, and had a particular fascination with the Philosopher's Stone, the legendary substance that was supposedly capable of turning base metals into gold. It was believed in Newton's day that all metals were compounds of sulfur and mercury, and that you could change one metal into another by changing the balance of these components. The Philosopher's Stone was said to be the catalyst needed for this transformation.

Authors who've studied the Newton manuscripts, such as Frank E. Manuel, describe the hundreds of pages of notes that Newton made from works about alchemy such as Elias Ashmole's *Theatrum Chemicum Britannicum* and Michael Maier's *Symbola Aureae Mensae Duodecim Nationum*.

Newton kept his interest in alchemy under wraps during his lifetime, as the making of gold and silver had been outlawed in England since the early fifteenth century. In Dan Brown's fictional account, the real reason for Newton's "high silence" was because the true secret of alchemy is that man is capable of godlike power, and this power would be dangerous in the wrong hands.

Robert Langdon declares Newton a Rosicrucian in Chapter 85 of *The Lost Symbol*. Although there's no evidence that Newton was ever a member of the society, he was certainly interested in it, and a copy of an English translation of *The Rosicrucian Manifestos* by Thomas Vaughan, entitled *The Fame and Confessions of the Fraternity R.C.*, was found in his library after his death. This story of a secret group of sages who were about to transform the landscape of Europe did much to inspire the popular fascination with alchemy of the seventeenth and eighteenth centuries, and was a major influence on the works of Elias Ashmole and Michael Maier.

Newton's interest in subjects that we now class as "occult" will come as a surprise to those who associate him purely with scientific rationalism. His manuscripts on subjects like alchemy and Rosicrucianism are a stark reminder that the distinction between science and superstition was still developing in the late seventeenth and early eighteenth centuries. It's no wonder that they appealed to Dan Brown, who loves to show us how the boundaries between things such as experimental science and mysticism are hazier than we think.

In Chapter 89 of *The Lost Symbol*, Katherine Solomon realizes that the phrase "all is revealed at the thirty-third degree" refers not just to the highest degree of the Scottish Rite, but to a temperature on the Newton Scale. This was a scale devised by Newton around the year 1700, which takes the temperature of melting ice as its "zeroth degree" and the temperature of boiling water as its 33rd degree, and was a precursor to the scale developed by the Swedish astronomer Anders Celsius in the middle of the eighteenth century. Katherine Solomon realizes that the capstone must be placed in boiling water, unveiling a further clue, "The secret hides within the Order Eight Franklin Square." But once again, these words will prove to have a cryptic double meaning.

See also: The Invisible College; Magic Squares.

Noetic Science

In Chapter 3 of *The Lost Symbol*, we learn that Katherine Solomon is a leading figure in Noetic Science. In Chapter 15, it's claimed that recent experiments at the Institute of Noetic Sciences in California have scientifically proved that human thought has the ability to change the physical world.

In an interview with the show *All Things Considered* on National Public Radio following the release of *The Lost Symbol*, Dan Brown revealed that he first became interested in Noetic Science when he was researching particle physics for *Angels and Demons*. Although Noetics wasn't relevant to that novel, he continued looking into the subject and was so intrigued that he decided to make it one of the main subjects of *The Lost Symbol*.

As Brown states at the front of his book, the Institute of Noetic Sciences is real, and is situated in Petaluma, north of San Francisco. A couple of days after the release of *The Lost Symbol*, they added an overview to the front page of their website to explain their work to readers of Brown's novel. They state that the word "noetic" is derived from the Greek word "noesis," which refers to an intuitive "inner knowing," and that their purpose is the clinical study of this:

> Noetic sciences bring objective scientific methods together with the deep wisdom of inner knowing to explore the mysteries of consciousness. Noetic sciences explore the "inner cosmos" of the mind (consciousness, soul, spirit) and how it relates to the "outer cosmos" of the physical world.

The institute was founded in 1973 by Paul N. Temple, who had previously worked for Exxon, and the astronaut Edgar Mitchell, whose interest in the universal consciousness of mankind was inspired by viewing the earth from space. Since it was founded, the institute has conducted work into the impact of consciousness on the physical world, exploring such things as the effects of prayer and meditation, the role of thought in healing, and the existence of a shared consciousness.

The laboratory at the institute includes a room that is electromagnetically shielded and nicknamed "the Cube," like Katherine Solomon's lab in the Smithsonian Museum Support Center. In it, they've conducted several of the experiments that Solomon describes, such as the impact of thought on water crystals. Many of their researchers explore the parallels between ancient mysticism and quantum theory, and some of them appeared in the 2004 film *What the Bleep Do We Know?*

As well as the activities of the institute, Dan Brown's treatment of Noetics in *The Lost Symbol* is heavily influenced by the writing of Lynne McTaggart, whose theories are credited as an influence on the work of Katherine Solomon in Chapter 15. McTaggart has published two major books in this area, *The Field*, which relates the mystical concept of the life force to the zero-point field of quantum mechanics, and *The Intention Experiment*, which purports to demonstrate how human thought and intention can change the physical world.

Many of the Noetic ideas Katherine Solomon refers to in *The Lost Symbol* are described in detail in McTaggart's books. In *The Field*, McTaggart describes how the Princeton Engineering Anomalies Research program monitored Random Event Generators to investigate the possibility of a global consciousness, detailing how the machines showed an unusually high degree of order during events such as the O. J. Simpson trial. In *The Intention Experiment*, she describes the effects of September 11, 2001, on Random Event Generators around the world, claiming that "the greatest variance in the machines away from randomness took place that day." She links this "coherent global horror" to the ancient belief in a "global consciousness" capable of changing the world. These findings are also described in Chapter 15 of *The Lost Symbol*, where we learn that Katherine has Random Event Generators in her lab.

In Chapter 84 of *The Lost Symbol*, Katherine tells Dean Galloway about experiments she's conducted that used charge-coupled device (CCD) cameras to photograph the energy transmitted from the fingertips of a faith healer, which she relates to the rays of light flowing from the hands of Jesus in a stained-glass window. This is a reference to the CCD camera experiments of Dr. Gary Schwartz from the University of Arizona, which McTaggart describes in *The Intention Experiment*. She claims that by using this sensitive equipment, Schwartz was able to photograph the rays of light coming from the healer's hands, and prove that the intention to heal has a physical manifestation in rays of light.

In Chapter 15, we find that Katherine's research into the power of focused thought has included such things as the study of the direction fish swim, chemical reactions in the body and the growth of plants. The experiment into how intention can affect the direction fish swim in is a reference to the work of Dr. William Braud, whose studies of the influence of intention on living things included one in which knife fish were monitored through electrodes attached to the side of a tank, as described in Chapter 7 of McTaggart's book *The Field*. The reference to chemical reactions in the body could refer to many of the experiments that McTaggart describes, such as the "biofeedback" experiments in which body functions such as blood pressure, heart rate and muscle tension are measured and relayed to a subject in real time. The reference to plant growth could refer to the "Germination Experiments," a series of studies that McTaggart ran in 2008 via her website in which participants were asked to send positive intentions to seeds to make them grow faster.

The ideas of McTaggart and the Institute of Noetic Sciences inform the note of optimism that concludes *The Lost Symbol*. For them, Noetic Science is proving what ancient religion always suggested, that mankind has the power to alter the tangible world with thought. When this power is unlocked, it will give humans the godlike ability to shape the world. Noetic writing is infused with the optimistic belief that humanity is about to enter a new age of enlightenment that Robert Langdon feels as he watches the sunrise from the U.S. Capitol at the end of the novel.

The fact that the Institute of Noetic Sciences is situated in the New Age hotspot of Northern California should have alerted readers to the possibility that Noetics is not the universally accepted scientific breakthrough that Dan Brown suggests. Far from having their worldview shaken by Noetics, many scientists would regard it as an exploitative hijacking of their terminology by New Age mystics. They would argue that "junk science" writers like Lynne McTaggart find proof that intention can change the physical world only because they're actively looking for it. The vast majority of scientific evidence would not lead us to believe that humans have psychic powers and can change the world with thought. But by giving general overviews of studies with anomalous outcomes, writers like McTaggart can advance their New Age agenda without making a rigorous effort to identify the real factors skewing the results.

The experiments of Noetic Science might sound exciting in the vague descriptions that Katherine Solomon gives, but they're not very convincing when you look into the details. There are no videos of subjects changing the direction of fish as if they were remote-control boats, just questionable analysis of electrical impulses. If any of these people really had evidence that thought can change the physical world, they'd be winning the Nobel Prize, not running healing workshops or selling DVDs from their website. The argument that all great truths were ridiculed when they were first proposed is a hugely unconvincing comeback. Lots of ideas have also been ridiculed for good reason. Just because ideas are strongly opposed doesn't necessarily mean they contain some counterintuitive wisdom that will eventually be accepted.

The truth is not that cutting-edge science is validating ancient wisdom, but that a New Age industry drawing analogies between science and mysticism has sprung up. A book about the power of prayer or meditation might not be attractive to a generation who has grown up with scientific skepticism. But rebrand prayer and meditation as "intent" and tie it in with oversimplified ideas from quantum mechanics such as the zero-point field, and readers can feel as if they're accepting scientific evidence rather than falling for mystical mumbo-jumbo.

Whatever the scientific validity of Noetics, it's not hard to imagine why it would have caught the attention of an author as popular as Dan Brown. In her review in the *New York Times*, Janet Maslin relates the Noetic idea of collective consciousness to the globally coordinated release of *The Lost Symbol*:

> One of the theories espoused by Dan Brown's new book is that when many people share the same thought, that thought can have physical effects. Let's test it on Tuesday. Watch what happens to bloggers, booksellers, nitpickers, code crackers, conspiracy theorists, fans and overheated search engines when *The Lost Symbol*, Mr. Brown's overdue follow-up to *Angels and Demons* (2000) and *The Da Vinci Code* (2003), finally sees the light of day.

This might indeed have been the reason why Dan Brown chose to write about Noetics. Knowing that his sequel to *The Da Vinci Code* would have one of the largest coordinated releases in history, with an initial print run of more than five million hardcovers, and simultaneous release as an audio book and e-book, he chose to make this kind of global synchronization the theme of his novel. This is why Katherine Solomon explains at the end of the book that the web of connected thought made possible by developments such as Twitter, Google and Wikipedia is turning the ancient concept of universal consciousness into a reality. In fact, "Dan Brown" became a trending topic on Twitter on the day of the book's release, with many fans tweeting "learning about Noetics" in reference to Katherine Solomon's prediction.

See also: Quantum Mysticism.

The Order of the Eastern Star

One of the reasons why Dan Brown's sympathetic treatment of the Freemasons was a surprise to many is that *The Da Vinci Code* portrayed the Catholic Church as a sexist institution that had intentionally repressed the sacred feminine. Freemasonry, as an all-male organization, was expected to be in line for similar criticism. In fact, Robert Langdon defends Freemasonry against such accusations when a member of the Harvard University Woman's Center asks him why women can't join the organization in Chapter 6 of *The Lost Symbol*. He tells her that Freemasonry is a male organization because its roots are in stonemasons' guilds, but that women are allowed to join a branch called The Order of the Eastern Star.

The Order of the Eastern Star is a group open to Master Masons and their wives and other female relatives. It was one of several groups related to Freemasonry that were created for women in the mid-nineteenth century, including the Order of the Amaranth, which also survives to this day. The Order of the Eastern Star was created by a lawyer and teacher called Dr.

Rob Morris, who wrote the order's ritual in about 1850, based on the stories of famous heroines from the Bible, such as Adah, Ruth, Esther, Martha and Electa. Although the ritual is similar to those of Freemasonry, it's not a direct rewrite, and offers just one initiation into the order, rather than the three degrees of Entered Apprentice, Fellow Craft and Master Mason that Masonry awards.

As outlined above, the ritual mentions biblical characters, but like Freemasonry the order is open to people of all religious persuasions, as long as they believe in a supreme being. As Langdon tells his Harvard students, the order still has more than a million members today, and is the largest fraternal organization in the world that both men and women can join.

See also: Freemasonry.

Paine, Thomas

In Chapter 131 of *The Lost Symbol*, Peter Solomon cites Thomas Paine as an example of a U.S. forefather with an unconventional attitude to the Bible. Paine was the Founding Father most closely associated with deism, and was the author of the radical pamphlet *The Age of Reason*.

Thomas Paine was born in 1737 in Thetford, a market town in Norfolk, England. He lived in England until he was thirty-seven, working as an excise officer. In 1774, he was introduced to Benjamin Franklin, who suggested he emigrate to America, and gave him a letter of recommendation. Paine arrived in Philadelphia later that year and took a job as editor of the *Pennsylvania Magazine* in January 1775. His pamphlet *Common Sense* was published a year later. It was a hit of Dan Brown–like proportions, selling more than 100,000 copies in a country with just 2 million free inhabitants.

Common Sense argued the case for independence from British rule in a powerful and accessible style. Although the ideas Paine was expressing weren't new, his concise prose style helped to incite widespread debate about independence and is thought to have influenced Thomas Jefferson when he wrote the Declaration of Independence.

In 1791, Paine set out his defense of the French Revolution in *The Rights of Man*, which argued that political revolution is permissible if a government doesn't safeguard the natural rights of its people. In 1793, he published the first part of *The Age of Reason*, which advocated deism, the belief in a supreme being based on observation of the natural world and reason, rather than organized religion. The book was extremely critical of the Christian Church, and argued that the events described in the Bible, such as the fall of man and the resurrection of Christ, were "fabulous inventions."

As with *Common Sense*, many of Paine's arguments had been put forward before, but his clear writing made them available to a mass audience. In the United States, the book went through seventeen editions and sold thousands of copies, and deism enjoyed a surge of popularity. However, a significant backlash followed, and many deeply critical responses were published. Some have suggested that Paine's controversial views on organized religion have meant that his status as a Founding Father has been significantly downplayed. Even today, many Americans would be surprised to find that a man who had such a huge impact on the founding of their nation held such strong anti-Christian beliefs.

Paine's account of Freemasonry was interestingly close to that given in *The Lost Symbol*. A manuscript found after his death entitled *An Essay on the Origin of Freemasonry* claims that the fraternity has its origins in ancient druidic religions, and is based on the worship of the sun. Paine claims that when Christianity overtook sun worship, the Druids feared persecution and decided to practice their secret rituals under the new name of the Masons. In his essay, he describes an oration given by Reverend William Dodd that detailed how ancient knowledge passed through the astronomers of Chaldea, the mystic kings of Egypt, the sages of Greece and the philosophers of Rome to the modern Freemasons. Like Peter Solomon, Paine doesn't give much concrete evidence for his claims, saying instead that this ancient revelation was deliberately kept secret.

See also: Ancient Mysteries; Deism; Jefferson, Thomas.

Pike, Albert

As he dashes through the House of the Temple to find Peter Solomon and Mal'akh in Chapter 121 of *The Lost Symbol*, Robert Langdon notices a bust of the nineteenth-century Freemason Albert Pike. A revered figure in the fraternity, and an attractive target for anti-Masonic theorists, Pike was instrumental in the development of Scottish Rite Freemasonry, which is central to the plot of Dan Brown's novel.

Born in Boston, Massachusetts, in 1809, Pike was accepted into Harvard but couldn't afford to go (which is a shame as he'd have done well on the symbology course). He worked as a schoolteacher from around 1825 to 1831, before moving to Arkansas. Pike became a Freemason in 1850, and just four years later he began a complete reworking of the Scottish Rite, the series of additional degrees that can be undertaken by a Master Mason. Pike is credited with giving the Scottish Rite the huge popularity it has today in the United States. He served as the Sovereign Grand Commander of the Scottish Rite's Southern Jurisdiction from 1859 until his death in 1891.

When the Civil War began, Pike served as a brigadier-general for the South. He formed a brigade of Native American soldiers, and fought at the Battle of Pea Ridge. It was alleged that Pike's troops scalped soldiers in the field, but the charges were later dropped due to lack of evidence.

It's sometimes claimed that Pike was one of the founders of the Ku Klux Klan, and in the early 1990s a group even petitioned the Council of the District of Columbia to remove a statue of him from Washington's Judiciary Square. There's no direct evidence for any of this, however. Although Pike was quoted as saying that he would leave Masonry rather than accept black people into it, this proves that he was guilty of unenlightened contemporary attitudes on race, but not that he was a Klan member.

Some have also linked Pike with the Knights of the Golden Circle, a secret society formed in the mid-nineteenth century, who wanted to annex a circle of territories in Mexico, Central America and the Caribbean to the U.S. as slave states. In their book *Shadow of the Sentinel*, Warren Getler and Bob Brewer argue that Pike intended to use the Scottish Rite to further the goals of the society and provoke a second U.S. civil war. They also allege that Pike was an undercover agent for the Knights of the Golden Circle who was entrusted with large quantities of gold following the defeat of the South in the Civil War. Their hugely unlikely account involves Pike enlisting Masons such as Jesse James to help him bury the treasure in a pattern determined by Masonic symbolism.

Albert Pike is to an extent responsible for popularizing the link between Freemasonry and the Ancient Mysteries that Peter

ABOVE: The Washington Monument. At the end of *The Lost Symbol*, Robert Langdon compares the monument's circular concourse to the ancient symbol of the circumpunct.

LAYING CORNER STONE, WASHINGTON MONUMENT

LEFT: Grand Master Benjamin B. French lays the cornerstone of the Washington Monument in a Masonic ceremony, July 4, 1848. The monument would not be completed until 1884.

ABOVE: Albrecht Dürer's 1514 engraving *Melencolia I*. The engraving features a notable magic square and provides Langdon with an important clue in *The Lost Symbol*.

RIGHT: The rows, columns, and diagonals of the square all add up to thirty-four, as do the four center squares, the four corner squares, and each of the quadrants.

ABOVE: Constantino Brumidi's fresco *The Apotheosis of Washington*, which is painted in the eye of the rotunda of the U.S. Capitol. Washington is seated in the center at the bottom of the inner circle; Benjamin Franklin is in the lower left-hand group, to the right of Minerva.

LEFT: The United States Capitol Building, for which George Washington laid the cornerstone in a Masonic ceremony in 1793.

ABOVE: The House of the Temple, the headquarters of the Scottish Rite of Freemasonry, Southern Jurisdiction, and the setting for the Prologue to *The Lost Symbol*.

RIGHT: Inside the House of the Temple. Robert Langdon admires the building's "symbolic ornamentation."

ABOVE: The Seal of Solomon superimposed over the Great Seal of the United States to produce an anagram of the word "mason." Langdon uses this to throw the CIA off his trail.

LEFT: Horatio Greenough's 1840 sculpture of George Washington, based on Phidias's statue of Zeus at Olympia. The sculpture, which weighs thirty tons, was once situated on the lawn of the U.S. Capitol (above, in a photograph taken in the 1890s) and is now in the National Museum of American History, Washington, D.C., part of the Smithsonian Institution.

ABOVE: George Washington's Masonic apron, which is displayed at the Grand Lodge of Pennsylvania in Philadelphia.

RIGHT: George Washington in full Masonic regalia. On his death in 1799, one of his aprons was buried with him.

ABOVE: James Sanborn's sculpture *Kryptos*, located in the courtyard outside the headquarters of the Central Intelligence Agency in Langley, Virginia. The sculpture is not directly mentioned until Chapter 127 of *The Lost Symbol*, but Brown makes a subtle reference to it at the very beginning of the novel.

RIGHT: Washington National Cathedral's notorious Darth Vader grotesque mentioned by Robert Langdon as he and Katherine Solomon arrive at the cathedral, having given the CIA the slip.

LEFT: The George Washington Masonic National Memorial in Alexandria, Virginia. Built in the 1920s, its aim was to express "the undying esteem of the Freemasons of the United States" for the country's first president.

"As the sun rose over Washington, Langdon looked to the heavens…" The Washington Monument and the U.S. Capitol at sunrise.

Solomon describes in *The Lost Symbol*, as he also believed the origins of Freemasonry were in pagan mysticism. But if ancient elements make it into Pike's writing, it's important to remember that his sources were the mythical embellishment of the original French authors of the Scottish Rite, and mystics such as Eliphas Lévi. Pike's works themselves are not proof that Freemasonry sprang from mysterious ancient roots.

Some anti-Masons have used Pike's writing to suggest a link between Freemasonry and Satanism. A late-nineteenth-century French hoaxer named Léo Taxil claimed that Pike's works encouraged Masons to worship the Devil, but this was based on a willful misinterpretation of the word "Lucifer." When Pike used the word, he was referring to the morning star, the planet Venus in its dawn appearance, and therefore to the search for enlightenment.

Pike died in 1891, and was buried in Oak Hill cemetery. In 1944, his remains were moved to the House of the Temple, the headquarters of the Southern Jurisdiction of the Scottish Rite. Thanks to his contributions to the Scottish Rite, Pike is still regarded as one of the most influential figures in American Freemasonry, and the fraternity's members continue to defend him against the accusations of conspiracy theorists.

See also: The House of the Temple; Satanism; The Scottish Rite.

Pyramids and Ancient Egypt

The plot of *The Lost Symbol* involves Robert Langdon following a series of clues inscribed on a Masonic pyramid he finds underneath the Capitol Building. In Chapter 30, Robert Langdon tells Director Sato that the pyramid is a common Masonic symbol, as the pyramid builders of ancient Egypt were the forerunners of the medieval stonemasons' guilds. The pyramid is probably the most famous symbol of the ancient world, and therefore an appropriate choice for a map revealing the location of the secret wisdom of all the ages. Pyramid-shaped structures were built by many ancient civilizations, including the Mesopotamians, the Nubians and the Greeks, not to mention Mesoamerican cultures such as the Maya. But it is the ancient Egyptians who are most associated with the structure.

More than 130 pyramids have been discovered in Egypt, many of which were built as tombs for the country's pharaohs. The best-known examples are the three pyramids in Giza, near Cairo, which date from around 2500 B.C. The oldest and largest of these was built for the Fourth Dynasty Egyptian King Khufu (Cheops in Greek), and is referred to as the Great Pyramid of Giza. It contains burial chambers known as the King's Chamber and the Queen's Chamber, as well as an unfinished chamber cut into the bedrock of the pyramid. These chambers are thought to have been built in alignment with certain stars that were significant to the ancient Egyptians, and the importance of these stars to the design of the pyramids has inspired alternative historians such as David Ovason to draw astrological links between ancient Egypt and Washington, D.C.

The pyramid is an important symbol in the Robert Langdon series. Chapter 1 of the first novel, *Angels and Demons*, starts with Robert Langdon having a nightmare about climbing the Great Pyramid of Giza. *The Da Vinci Code* ends with Langdon staring up at the stars through the Pyramide Inversée in the Louvre in Paris, neatly foreshadowing the role that pyramids will play in the third Langdon book.

In Masonic theory, the pyramid symbolizes the link between the fraternity and ancient Egypt. While there's no evidence of a genuine historical connection, there's certainly evidence that the link has long been a part of Masonry's mythic history. A reference to Egypt can be found in the oldest Masonic document in existence, *The Regius Manuscript*, which is dated to about 1390. This 794-line poem, thought to be based on earlier documents that are now lost, outlines the rules of medieval stonemasonry and claims that the craft can be traced back to ancient Egypt. It tells of how the Alexandrian mathematician Euclid founded Freemasonry in Egypt and was the first Master

Mason. It then details how King Athelstan, the grandson of Alfred the Great, imported Freemasonry to England in the tenth century.

The association with ancient Egypt remained important to Masonry as lodges began to admit non-stonemasons in the sixteenth and seventeenth centuries, and the shift from operative to speculative Freemasonry occurred. When the Reverend James Anderson published *The Constitutions of the Free-Masons* in 1723, he elaborated on the idea that Freemasonry existed in ancient Egypt, making specific mention of the "famous pyramids."

Around the time Anderson published his *Constitutions*, there was a lot of excitement about ancient Egypt, and the possible meanings of hieroglyphics, which would not be understood until the successful translation of the Rosetta Stone in the early nineteenth century. In 1713, French author Jean Terrasson published a novel called *Sethos*, describing the powerful teachings of the Ancient Mystery Schools of Egypt. In keeping with the conventions of historical fantasy, Terrasson pretended that the work was a translation of an ancient lost manuscript written by mysterious Egyptian priests. The hoax worked, and many believed the myth that these Ancient Mystery Schools were the predecessors of the Freemasons (perhaps this novel is the "indisputable evidence" of secret ancient wisdom that Robert Langdon makes a vague reference to in Chapter 30).

The supposed link between Freemasonry and ancient Egypt inspired many rogue Masonic groups in the eighteenth and nineteenth centuries. In 1776, an Italian calling himself Count

Alessandro di Cagliostro (whose real name was Giuseppe Balsamo) established the Mother Lodge for the Adjustment of the High Egyptian Masonry, which was known as the "Egyptian Rite." Cagliostro opened Egyptian lodges in England, France and Germany before being arrested in Rome in 1789 and finding himself condemned to death for heresy. The sentence was subsequently reduced to life imprisonment, and Cagliostro died in prison in 1795. The story of Cagliostro inspired works by notable writers such as Friedrich Schiller, Johann Wolfgang Goethe and Alexandre Dumas.

Ancient Egypt continued to fire the imaginations of nineteenth-century Masons, inspiring rogue appendant groups such as the Rite of Memphis and the Rite of Mizraim in France. Although neither was officially recognized, they each devised more than ninety additional degrees to reveal how Freemasons were the secret guardians of ancient Egyptian knowledge.

The idea that Freemasonry had inherited the wisdom of ancient Egypt was explored by the esoteric writer Manly P. Hall in works such as *Freemasonry of the Ancient Egyptians*. In the lore of conspiracy theorists, the complex work of writers such as Hall was simplified into the idea that the pyramid is a secret Masonic symbol. This is then taken to show that the pyramid on the Great Seal of the U.S. proves that the Masons wish to take over the world, or that the capstone on the Washington Monument proves that America's Masonic Founding Fathers secretly worshipped Egyptian deities.

In fact, while the pyramid is an important symbol to anti-Masonic conspiracy theorists, it is not especially important to modern Masons. If you ask a Freemason today which symbols are important to the craft, he might tell you about the square and compass, the pillars of Jachin and Boaz and the winding staircase, but he is unlikely to mention pyramids or the secret wisdom of ancient Egypt.

See also: Ancient Mysteries; The Great Seal of the United States; The Washington Monument.

Quantum Mysticism

The two previous Robert Langdon novels, *Angels and Demons* and *The Da Vinci Code*, have taken the conflict between science and religion as their major theme. Through his depiction of the Catholic Church and of historical figures such as Galileo, Copernicus and Leonardo da Vinci, Brown dramatized the conflict that occurs when experimental proof contradicts belief.

His depiction of the relationship between science and religion takes a more positive turn in *The Lost Symbol*. Through the character of Peter Solomon, Brown discusses several parallels between modern science and ancient belief. In doing so, he touches on a vast field of pseudoscience that has been called "quantum mysticism." ·

As Peter Solomon points out to his sister Katherine in Chapter 15 of *The Lost Symbol*, several of the founders of quantum mechanics, such as Heisenberg and Schrödinger, had an interest in mysticism, so the two fields might not be as disparate as assumed. But many modern scientists object to the

New Age hijacking of quantum physics, and dismiss the trend as "junk science."

The term "quantum mysticism" is used to describe ideas that blend ancient mysticism and quantum mechanics which have recently become popular in New Age circles.

One of the most influential books in the movement was Fritjof Capra's 1975 bestseller *The Tao of Physics: An Exploration of the Parallels Between Modern Physics and Eastern Mysticism*. In it, Capra draws several of the parallels between modern physics and ancient wisdom that Peter Solomon points out to Katherine in *The Lost Symbol*. He makes the link between subatomic polarity and the dual world described in the Hindu scripture the *Bhagavadgita*, and draws the connection between the unity of all things known as Brahman in Hinduism, Dharmakaya in Buddhism and Tao in Taoism and the unity at the subatomic level suggested by modern physics:

> The basic oneness of the universe is not only the central characteristic of the mystic universe, but is one of the most important revelations of modern physics. It becomes apparent at the atomic level, and manifests itself more and more as one penetrates deeper down into matter, down into the realm of subatomic particles.

The quantum mysticism genre's next hit was Gary Zukav's *The Dancing Wu Li Masters*, which was published in 1979, and is one of the books in Peter Solomon's library in *The Lost Symbol*. Since then, popular additions to the genre have included Deepak Chopra's *Quantum Healing*, Michael Talbot's *The Holographic Universe* and Arnold Mindell's *Quantum Mind and Healing*.

The movement hit the big screen with the 2004 film *What the Bleep Do We Know?*, which was picked up by a major distributor and was a surprise box-office hit. Blending interviews with physicists, neurosurgeons and several members of the Institute of Noetic Sciences with narrative segments starring deaf actress Marlee Matlin, the film explored such things as how the human mind can affect physical reality.

While it has created a thriving New Age subgenre, quantum mysticism has irritated many physicists, who argue that the movement is based on coincidental similarities of language rather than genuine connections. They claim that the spurious links to quantum mechanics made in New Age writing are nothing but an appeal to the vanity of readers, who think that a paperback bought from a shop selling crystals and dream-catchers is a shortcut to understanding complex theories that require years of study of advanced mathematics.

By the same token, some mystics have questioned why a scientific parallel is needed to legitimize their beliefs. They argue that quantum mystics want their spiritual beliefs backed up by physics only because they can't abandon the scientific worldview they're steeped in.

At any rate, it's no surprise that these ideas found their way into the work of Dan Brown, whose success can also be seen as a sign of our enduring fascination with religious belief in an age of scientific skepticism.

See also: Noetic Science.

The Rosicrucians

In Chapter 85 of *The Lost Symbol*, Robert Langdon mentions the Rosicrucians to Katherine Solomon, who reveals that she's read their manifestos as part of her research.

The legend of the Rosicrucians derives from three books published in early seventeenth-century Germany that were supposedly written in the mid-fifteenth century by a monk named Christian Rosenkreuz, who had acquired secret wisdom in Damascus, Egypt and Morocco before returning to Europe. The books told the story of Rosenkreuz's pilgrimages and how he formed "The Fraternity of the Rose Cross," which consisted of eight monks who undertook an oath to seek knowledge, heal the sick, and find successors to replace them when they died. The story went that three generations of these monks had passed, and they were now willing to share their knowledge of alchemy, magic, Kabbalah and ancient Egyptian mysticism.

The manifestos gained massive popularity in early-seventeenth-century Europe, and more than 400 pamphlets and books were published about them. The idea that a secret brotherhood of sages was about to transform the intellectual landscape of Europe with their ancient wisdom caused huge excitement and fueled the mood of utopianism.

Rosenkreuz, however, never existed. He was probably the invention of a German Lutheran minister named Johann Valentin Andrae, although as Dean Galloway points out, some believe he was actually Sir Francis Bacon under a pseudonym. But whether they were genuine or not, the documents were hugely influential, and led to the formation of several Rosicrucian societies. Some of these still exist today, such as the Ancient and Mystical Order Rosae Crucis, which claims to have more than a quarter of a million members (you can join at www.amorc.org if you like).

The symbol of the rose and the cross was brought to popularity by the fad, and appears in Degrees 15 to 18 of the Scottish Rite of Freemasonry, which are collectively known as "The Chapter of Rose Croix."

Though it would be inaccurate to claim that Freemasonry grew out of Rosicrucianism, the order is thought to have been popular with many of the speculative Freemasons of the seventeenth century such as Elias Ashmole. It's not hard to imagine how the utopianism of the Rosicrucian fad might have influenced the ideals of brotherhood and self-improvement that developed in speculative Freemasonry.

Rosenkreuz might not have existed, but the ideals he represented struck a chord, and had a significant impact on nascent speculative Freemasonry.

See also: Ancient Mysteries; Bacon, Francis; The Invisible College; The Scottish Rite; Utopia.

Satanism

In Chapter 23 of *The Lost Symbol*, Langdon refers to one of the most enduring and ludicrous myths about Freemasonry, which is that it's a front for Devil worship.

Unlike some misconceptions that have built up around Freemasonry, this one began as a deliberate hoax by late-nineteenth-century French author Léo Taxil, who was born Marie Joseph Gabriel Antoine Jogand-Pagès in Marseilles in 1854.

In the 1890s Taxil masterminded an elaborate lie to mock both Freemasonry and the Catholic Church. Feigning a conversion to Catholicism, he authored a series of sensationalist works about the fraternity that revealed their shocking participation in Satanism. He claimed that the influential Mason Albert Pike presided over sexual orgies worshipping the goat-headed pagan deity Baphomet, who had been popularized by the work of occultist Eliphas Lévi.

Some of Taxil's "exposés" relied on the accounts of a woman called Diana Vaughan, who had supposedly been impregnated by Satan during an orgy. Taxil promised to reveal this unlikely eyewitness at a lecture in 1897, only to admit to the gathered crowd that the accounts had been wholly fictitious.

Even though Taxil revealed his entire project to be untrue, the link between Satanism and Freemasonry has lingered in the overactive imaginations of conspiracy theorists. The myth that Albert Pike was referring to the Devil rather than the morning star when he wrote of "Lucifer the light-bearer" has persisted, and Christian fundamentalists still produce frenzied works such as *Masonry: Beyond the Light*, in which born-again William Schnoebelen claims that he was possessed by demons and inducted into an army of Satanic slaves as he progressed through the degrees of Freemasonry. Which certainly beats the Rotary Club if you're looking for something to do with your evenings.

A figure who did much to cement the false association of Freemasonry with Satanism was Aleister Crowley, the occultist who we find was an inspiration to Mal'akh in Chapter 77. As Crowley's defenders are quick to point out, he wasn't really a Satanist, as he founded his own religion called Thelema, based on the dictum "Do what thou wilt shall be the whole of the law." But he did engage in ceremonies of "sex magick," join witches' covens and popularize Tarot cards and Ouija boards, so he would hardly have been up there with George Washington as a shining example of the virtues of the fraternity.

Thankfully for the Freemasons, Crowley was never a member of a legitimate lodge, although he joined unrecognized Masonic groups in Mexico and France. He also took over a group called the Ordo Templi Orientis in 1910, when he converted its founder, Theodore Reuss, to Thelema. He rewrote the rituals of the organization, incorporating some of the symbolism and language of Freemasonry. Although Crowley claimed these rituals were an extension of Masonic degrees, most Masons vehemently rejected any connection with someone famously denounced as "the wickedest man in the world." Nonetheless, the association lingered, and photos of Crowley in Masonic dress are still trotted out as proof that the fraternity are secret Devil worshippers.

The imagined link between Freemasonry and Satanism has even extended to theories about the Founding Fathers and Washington, D.C., As one of Langdon's students points out in Chapter 6, some theorists have spotted secret Satanic signs in the city's street plan, such as the inverse pentagram above the White House.

Further misconceptions have derived from the supposed connection with Satanism, such as the myth that stripping naked and riding around on a goat are part of a Masonic initiation ceremony. It's pretty safe to say that these activities, which sound more like a particularly painful example of college fraternity hazing, are not going on behind the closed doors of your local lodge.

See also: Freemasonry; Pike, Albert; Washington, D.C.

The Scottish Rite

A recurring element in *The Lost Symbol* is the thirty-third degree of Scottish Rite Freemasonry. When explaining the meaning of Peter Solomon's ring to Director Sato, Robert Langdon mentions that the thirty-third degree exists solely within the Scottish Rite, but the hierarchy of Masonic degrees is so complex that he doesn't want to go into any detail about them. It's understandable that Brown doesn't want to slow the action down by piling on even more exposition, but it should be noted that the Scottish Rite is just one of many appendant organizations available to Freemasons.

While "pure and ancient Freemasonry" is defined as the three degrees of Entered Apprentice, Fellow Craft and Master Mason, there are a number of rites that offer further degrees of education. In the U.S., the two major appendant bodies are known as the York Rite and the Scottish Rite. The York Rite takes its name from *The Regius Manuscript* of around 1390 and confers ten additional degrees, which are grouped into Royal Arch Degrees, Cryptic Mason Degrees and Chivalric

Orders. The Scottish Rite, officially known as the Ancient and Accepted Scottish Rite of Freemasonry, was developed in the eighteenth century by Andrew Michael Ramsay, a Scottish Mason who lived in Paris, and rewritten by Albert Pike in his 1868 book *Morals and Dogma*.

The Scottish Rite awards a total of thirty-two degrees, plus a thirty-third degree which is bestowed by the supreme council on those individuals who have made important contributions to Masonry. The mysterious nature of this final degree has inspired much anti-Masonic theory.

The thirty-three degrees of the Scottish Rite are grouped into four divisions, which vary between the Southern Masonic Jurisdiction (SMJ) and the Northern Masonic Jurisdiction (NMJ). The former stays closest to the rituals devised by Albert Pike, so I'll give an overview of these.

As mentioned, the Scottish Rite is additional to the three standard Masonic degrees of Entered Apprentice, Fellow Craft and Master Mason, so it begins with the fourth degree. The degrees numbered from 4 to 14 are entitled "The Lodge of Perfection." These rituals tell the legend of Hiram Abiff through dramatic reenactments of events such as his murder and the trial of his killers.

The next four degrees are known as the Chapter of Rose Croix, and deal with the rebuilding of King Solomon's Temple. This name has inspired many conspiracy theorists to connect the Freemasons and the Rosicrucians, the seventeenth-century utopian movement that was said to have been founded by a German monk called Christian Rosenkreuz, although the symbol of the rose and the cross was in use long before then.

Degrees 19 to 30 are known as the Council of Kadosh. They are more abstract rituals, instructing Masons in qualities such as fellowship, compassion, tolerance, understanding and reason, and emphasizing the goal of constant self-improvement.

Degrees 31 and 32 are known as the Consistory Degrees, and they outline the need for constant self-examination and the nature of true brotherhood. As mentioned above, the thirty-third degree of the Scottish Rite can't be requested, but is awarded by the Supreme Council for exceptional contributions to Freemasonry. The mysterious nature of this degree has inspired many conspiracy theories. There are very few thirty-third-degree Masons, as the Supreme Council selects only thirty-three of them from any region at any time. This has led some to suggest that the majority of Masons have no idea of the fraternity's real agenda, and that only carefully selected thirty-third-degree Masons are aware of the true goal of overturning religion and government to establish a New World Order.

You'd think that the publication of *The Lost Symbol* would be a good opportunity for these thirty-third-degree Masons to rise up and impose this New World Order they're so keen on, so by the time you read this we'll probably be in thrall to our new Masonic overlords. Or perhaps they'll wait for the novel to come out in paperback.

Although his treatment of the Scottish Rite in *The Lost Symbol* is generally respectful, Dan Brown does add a few sensationalist embellishments here and there. For example, in the book's Prologue, straight after claiming that all rituals in the novel are real, he depicts a Scottish Rite ceremony in which wine is sipped from a real human skull. Human skulls are not used in any modern Masonic ritual, although there are records of renegade groups who included such macabre practices in their rituals, such as the "Cerneau" group in the nineteenth century, who were never officially recognized by the fraternity. So if you're thinking of visiting your local lodge, it's probably better to be on the safe side and leave your human skull collection at home.

See also: Freemasons; Pike, Albert; The Rosicrucians; Solomon's Temple; Thirty-three.

The Shriners

When the Masonic pyramid reveals the clue "The secret hides within the Order Eight Franklin Square," Director Sato visits Washington's Franklin Square to find which order this is referring to. She assumes that it must be pointing to the Almas Shrine Temple, the building of the Ancient Arabic Order of Nobles of the Mystic Shrine, better known as "The Shriners."

The Ancient Arabic Order of Nobles of the Mystic Shrine is an appendant body of Freemasonry, like the York Rite and the Scottish Rite. As with other appendant bodies, you need to join a lodge and complete the degrees of Entered Apprentice, Fellow Craft and Master Mason in order to be eligible to join. Unlike the York Rite and the Scottish Rite, however, it doesn't offer additional degrees of Freemasonry.

The Shriners were established in 1870 by two Masons named Billy Florence and Dr. Walter Fleming, who reckoned that Freemasonry was getting too serious and losing its sense of fun. Florence was an actor who had seen a musical comedy about a Middle Eastern secret society and he decided to create a new fraternity for Masons with an Arabic theme. Accordingly, their official headgear was to be a red fez with a black tassel and an emblem of a crescent, scimitar and sphinx (thankfully, Dan Brown doesn't try to rope all this into the theory that Freemasonry has its origins in the Mystery Schools of ancient Egypt). Eventually, the group caught on, and by the turn of the century it had more than 50,000 members.

Members of the Shrine are known as "nobles," and their initiation ceremony includes a symbolic crossing of the hot sands of the desert. The Shriners have built several large temples in the Moorish revival style, which often feature Middle Eastern touches such as domes and minarets. They include the "Mecca Temple" at 56th Street and 6th Avenue in New York, now the New York City Center, the "Mosque" in Richmond, Virginia, which is now known as the Landmark Theater, and the Al Malaikah Shrine Auditorium in Los Angeles, which hosted the Academy Awards before they moved to the Kodak Theatre.

Washington, D.C.'s Almas Shrine Temple also has a Middle Eastern façade, with pointed arches and terra-cotta tiles, which is why the building resembles an ancient mosque to Turner Simpkins in Chapter 99 of *The Lost Symbol*. Although the original Almas Shrine Temple was built in 1929, it's been in its current location only since 1990, when it moved to make way for the Franklin Square office complex. The restoration firm Graciano has a case study of the Almas Shrine project on their website, detailing how they painstakingly dismantled, repaired and reassembled the 35,000 pieces of the building's terra-cotta façade. Inside the new temple are offices, meeting rooms and a large ballroom.

In recent years, the Shriners have toned down some of their Middle Eastern theme, such as the references to Islam in its ceremonies. What might have seemed exotic and fun in the nineteenth century could now be seen as a mockery of Islam at an especially sensitive time.

As Turner Simpkins notes when Director Sato tells him about the Almas Shrine Temple, the organization is best known for its philanthropic work, especially the building of children's hospitals. The first of these was built in Shreveport, Louisiana, in 1920 following the polio epidemic of 1919. There are now twenty-two Shriner hospitals in the United States, Mexico and Canada that provide free care to children regardless of race, religion or relationship to the fraternity. Historically, they specialized in orthopedic care, but they now deal with all pediatric cases, and have been called the greatest example of Masonic philanthropy.

Like the George Washington Masonic National Memorial and the anagram of the word "Mason" on the Great Seal of the United States, the main function of the Almas Shrine Temple in *The Lost Symbol* is to misdirect the reader. While "The Ancient Arabic Order of Nobles of the Mystic Shrine" might sound like the kind of group who would guard the lost secrets of the Egyptian Mystery Schools, anyone familiar with the Shriners will have guessed they were a red herring.

See also: Freemasonry; The Order of the Eastern Star; The Scottish Rite.

The Smithsonian Museum Support Center

In Chapter 3 of *The Lost Symbol*, we find that Robert Langdon's mentor, Peter Solomon, is currently serving as head of the Smithsonian Institution. Later we learn that he's provided his sister Katherine with a sealed laboratory in the Smithsonian Museum Support Center (SMSC) in Suitland, outside Washington, D.C., so she can conduct her Noetic experiments.

The Smithsonian Institution is an educational and research institute that runs nineteen museums, nine research centers and the National Zoo. It was founded when the British scientist James Smithson left his estate to the U.S. government in his will in the early nineteenth century. The Smithsonian Institution Building was constructed between 1847 and 1855, and is situated on the National Mall, along with ten other Smithsonian museums, including the National Museum of American History, the National Museum of Natural History and the National Gallery of Art.

The SMSC was opened in May 1983 to allow off-site preservation and study of the huge collections of museums like the National Museum of Natural History and the National Museum of American History. It consists of five large "pods," connected by a corridor known as "the street," and houses more than fifty-five million items across twelve miles of storage cabinets.

Although Pod 5 contains Katherine's lab in *The Lost Symbol*, it is the "wet pod" in the real SMSC, housing twenty-five million specimens from the National Museum of Natural History's biological collections, including the giant squid that Trish shows Mal'akh in Chapter 37. It was opened in 2007 at the east of the SMSC site, adding a further 125,000 square feet to the complex.

The SMSC was the first of *The Lost Symbol*'s locations to be hinted at on NBC's *Today Show* in the run-up to the novel's release. Host Matt Lauer challenged viewers to identify the location, mentioning that it's been nicknamed the "Death Star" as it contains specimens of dead animals. So many viewers searched online to find the answer that a scam was set up to trap them. Shortly after the show aired, the top result on Google for "death star research" would take you to a "scareware" site that pretends a virus has infected your computer and you need to pay for anti-virus software to eliminate it. Perhaps if Dan Brown had spent less time warning his fans about the Illuminati and more time warning them about online scammers, this distressing situation would never have occurred.

See also: Noetic Science; Solomon, Katherine.

Solomon, Katherine

An important part of the Dan Brown formula is that a beautiful woman who's just had a close relative kidnapped or murdered must be drawn into the treasure hunt. She must also be educated enough to discuss the novel's esoteric and scientific themes with Robert Langdon rather than saying something like, "Shut up about the Rosicrucians and help me find my brother before his other hand gets chopped off."

After Vittoria Vetra in *Angels and Demons* and Sophie Neveu in *The Da Vinci Code*, we get Katherine Solomon in *The Lost Symbol*. We are introduced to Katherine in Chapter 5, where we learn that she's fifty years old, has black hair and olive skin, and is a leading researcher in the field of Noetic Science. We find that she's published two books on the subject, and has recently made a series of breakthroughs that will bring Noetics to worldwide prominence.

Dan Brown's characters are often a composite of several real people, but there are two women in particular who can claim to be the inspiration for Katherine Solomon: Lynne McTaggart and Marilyn Schlitz.

Lynne McTaggart, who is mentioned in Chapter 15 of *The Lost Symbol*, has written extensively about the science of consciousness and the power of group thought in her books *The Field* and *The Intention Experiment*. In a blog posted a couple of days after the release of *The Lost Symbol*, McTaggart wrote about the surreal experience of finding her work referenced in such a popular book:

> Every so often my life takes such a fantastical turn that I am overwhelmed by the feeling that I am actually in the midst of a lucid dream, and that any moment awakening will hand me back my ordinary world. I had that feeling yesterday when I got an email from my editor informing me that my book *The Intention Experiment*, my website: www.theintentionexperiment.com and a good deal of my research were named, explained and used as the background source of a major plotline in Dan Brown's new book.

The other major influence on the character seems to be Marilyn Schlitz, the president of the Institute of Noetic Sciences, who has also conducted research into the powers of consciousness. Like Lynne McTaggart, she posted a blog entry about the character shortly after the publication of *The Lost Symbol*:

> As I read *The Lost Symbol* with mounting fascination, I am pondering what it means to become a fictional character in a book that

has captured the collective imagination like wildfire on a hot summer day.

Schlitz certainly has strong grounds to believe she's the inspiration for the character. Like Katherine Solomon, she conducts clinical studies into the power of the mind to change the physical world in an electromagnetically shielded room nicknamed "the Cube." Like Katherine Solomon, she has published her findings in two books, *Living Deeply* and *Consciousness and Healing*. And in what's probably just a strange coincidence, Schlitz mentions in her blog post that both her father and her brother were thirty-second-degree Scottish Rite Masons, and that her father passed a Masonic ring down to her brother after his death. Fortunately for her, though, she's never been pursued by a tattooed psychopath who's really (SPOILER ALERT!!!) her nephew.

I find it highly suspicious that two women who've dedicated their professional lives to making their thoughts change the external world have been portrayed so positively by the world's biggest writer. In fact, the reams of free publicity that both Lynne McTaggart and the Institute of Noetic Sciences get in *The Lost Symbol* are more convincing evidence that sending out positive vibes can affect such things as Dan Brown's laptop than any of the experiments they've conducted.

See also: Langdon, Robert; Mal'akh; Noetic Science.

Solomon's Temple

When Robert Langdon watches Mal'akh's secret video in Chapter 117 of *The Lost Symbol*, he sees that it contains a reenactment of the murder of Hiram Abiff, the architect of King Solomon's Temple. This temple is what gives Freemasonry its central narrative, and inspired the surname of Peter and Katherine Solomon.

According to the biblical legend, King Solomon's Temple was built in Jerusalem. The story goes that King David intended to build a vast temple on Mount Moriah, which is now known as Temple Mount. Before his death he collected vast quantities of gold and silver so that his son, Solomon, could build the temple. Solomon asked for help from the Phoenician King of Tyre, who responded by sending a highly skilled man called Hiram, who is known as Hiram Abiff in Masonic lore.

In the biblical accounts (the story is told slightly differently in the Books of Chronicles and the Books of Kings), the worker known as Hiram completes his work successfully. However, in the Masonic version, Hiram Abiff is murdered just as work on the temple is nearing completion. In their account, Abiff was in charge of more than 150,000 workers, who were divided into ranks of Entered Apprentice, Fellow Craft and Master Mason. One of Abiff's duties was to decide when workers were skilled enough to rise up a rank. These workers would be given a secret password to identify their rank to the wages clerk. A group of fifteen workers supposedly devised a plot to threaten to kill Abiff unless he raised them to the rank of Master Mason and revealed the secret password. Twelve conspirators then dropped out, leaving just three handily alliterative workers—Jubela, Jubelo and Jubelum.

These three confronted Abiff with their ultimatum. Abiff refused, and Jubela slashed his throat with a measuring gauge. Jubelo then attacked him with an architect's square, before Jubelum finished him off by hitting him on the head with a gavel.

Abiff's last words before he died were apparently "Is there no help for the widow's son?"—a phrase that is still used as a plea by Freemasons, as in Warren Bellamy's request for help from Dean Galloway in *The Lost Symbol*. One of the earliest indications Dan Brown fans had that the third Robert Langdon book would involve the Masons was when this plea was hidden on the dust jacket of *The Da Vinci Code*.

The twelve workers who had earlier backed out of the plan confessed to King Solomon, wearing white aprons to demonstrate that there was no blood on their hands. Jubela, Jubelo and Jubelum were then captured and killed.

This story gives Freemasonry many of its most important symbols, such as the measuring gauge, architect's square, gavel and apron. It has also inspired rituals such as Degrees 4 to 14 of the Scottish Rite, which involve reenactments of the murder of Abiff and the trial of his killers.

Temple Mount, where Solomon's Temple is believed to have been situated, is one of the most fought-over religious sites in the world. For Judaism, it's the spot where the world was created and expanded to its current form, and where God collected the dust he used to fashion the first man, Adam. It's also the setting for such biblical events such as God's commandment to Abraham to kill his only son, Isaac. For Islam, the mount is the place from where Mohammed ascended to heaven, as well as the location of the al-Aqsa Mosque and the oldest existing Islamic building, the Dome of the Rock.

See also: Pike, Albert; The Scottish Rite; The Widow's Son.

Thirty-three (33)

In the second chapter of *The Lost Symbol*, we learn that Mal'akh has ascended to the thirty-third degree, which is described as the "highest echelon" of Freemasonry.

In fact, the thirty-third degree occurs in a particular appendant body of Freemasonry known as the Scottish Rite. The Scottish Rite awards additional degrees of Freemasonry that follow on from the three foundational degrees of Entered Apprentice, Fellow Craft and Master Mason. It awards a total of thirty-two degrees, but it can also bestow a thirty-third degree on those who've shown particular devotion to the fraternity. Very few Masons are raised to the thirty-third degree, and the mysterious, select nature of this has made the degree attractive to conspiracy theorists. Some have claimed that it's only when you receive the thirty-third degree that you are told the true Masonic agenda of establishing a New World Order.

Although Dan Brown is understandably simplifying the details of Freemasonry, it's inaccurate to claim that the thirty-third degree is the fraternity's highest. It might be the highest of the additional degrees offered by the Scottish Rite, but the highest degree of Freemasonry itself is the third degree, that of Master Mason. Also, as the thirty-third degree is awarded as an honor to Masons who have distinguished themselves, Mal'akh cannot have ascended to it in the ritual described in the Prologue, as he claims in Chapter 2. Despite Brown's claim at the front of the novel that all the rituals described in it are real, he gives a highly fictionalized account of them right from the start.

Nonetheless, the number 33 is deeply significant for Brown's take on Freemasonry, and it recurs throughout the novel's 133 chapters. The Prologue starts at 8:33 p.m. in the Temple Room, which contains a thirty-three-foot-high throne; the number 33 appears on Peter Solomon's Masonic ring; and the weight of the Washington Monument's capstone is given as thirty-three hundred pounds. On page 333 of the hardcover edition of *The Lost Symbol* (page 33 would have been more impressive), Robert Langdon and Katherine Solomon discuss the importance of the number in numerology, and explain how it has significance in Christianity and Islam as well as Freemasonry.

When the release of *The Lost Symbol* was set at September 15, 2009 (09/15/09), there was much speculation on blogs and message boards about the relevance of the date, and the events of Masonic significance that had taken place on it. However, as so often with Dan Brown, the puzzle was much simpler than everyone was assuming. When thelostsymbol.com went live, the loading page revealed that 9 + 15 + 9 = 33.

See also: Freemasonry; Pike, Albert; The Scottish Rite.

The United States Capitol

The Lost Symbol begins with Robert Langdon being summoned to the United States Capitol to give a lecture, only to find the severed hand of his mentor, Peter Solomon, pointing to Constantino Brumidi's *The Apotheosis of Washington*, which is painted in the eye of the Capitol's rotunda.

The United States Capitol, sometimes called the Capitol Building, is the meeting place of the United States Congress. It's situated on top of Capitol Hill, at the eastern end of the National Mall in Washington, D.C.

The location for the Capitol Building was chosen by Pierre Charles L'Enfant when he was devising his plan for the new capital city of the United States. He picked a site on Jenkins Hill, overlooking a broad vista.

In the world of conspiracy theory, L'Enfant is thought to have selected the site as part of a Masonic square and compass shape in the Washington street plan, with the Capitol Building as the top of the compass and the legs leading down Pennsylvania Avenue to the White House and, rather less continuously, down Maryland Avenue to the Jefferson Memorial. The square is then traced either from the White House to the Lincoln Memorial to the Jefferson Memorial or along Canal Street and Louisiana Avenue. However, despite what Robert Langdon tells his students, L'Enfant wasn't a Mason, and wouldn't have had any particular reason to hide such shapes in his plan.

L'Enfant was appointed to design the Capitol Building, but was fired from the project following disagreements with commissioners, and refused to hand over his plans. To find a new design, Thomas Jefferson decided to hold a competition. The winner was an amateur architect called William Thornton, and after several modifications to his plan, construction began.

As Robert Langdon notes, the cornerstone of the building was laid by George Washington on September 18, 1793, in an overtly Masonic ceremony. Washington marched from the future site of the president's house and along the road that would become Pennsylvania Avenue to a trench that had been dug on Jenkins Hill, accompanied by members of several local lodges. Wearing his Masonic apron, Washington stepped into the trench and placed a ceremonial silver plate on the cornerstone. The plate was then anointed with the traditional Masonic offerings of corn, wine and oil. A silver trowel was used to spread cement on the stone, which was then tapped with a marble gavel.

According to Masonic lore, corn, wine and oil are symbols of abundance, good health and contentment respectively. They are also said to represent the wages paid to workers at King Solomon's Temple in the story of Hiram Abiff.

The tradition of offering corn, wine and oil dates back earlier than Freemasonry, however. Some conspiracy buffs have sought to portray them as sacrifices to appease pagan gods, evidence of how the "Masonic Republic" of the U.S. deliberately undermined Christianity. In one unlikely account, the offering of corn is seen as a sign that the entire Masonic ceremony is in truth dedicated to Dagon, the Phoenician god of corn.

The Lost Symbol ends with Robert Langdon back in the Capitol Building. Standing at the pinnacle of the Capitol Dome, he looks out at the Washington Monument as the sun rises and recalls New Age ideas about the imminent enlightenment of man.

See also: The Apotheosis of Washington; Washington, George; Washington, D.C.

Utopia

At several points in *The Lost Symbol*, such as when Robert Langdon is arriving in Washington, and when Peter Solomon is lecturing at the Phillips Exeter Academy, it's claimed that the founding of the United States of America was a utopian project.

"Utopia" is the name given to an ideal society or community. The term is taken from the title of Sir Thomas More's 1516 book, which describes a fictional island in the Atlantic Ocean. The tradition of utopian writing goes back much further than this, however, most notably to Plato's dialogue *The Republic*, written in approximately 380 B.C.

The idea that the U.S. was established as an idyll in the new territories is central to many theories about the Founding Fathers. The utopian tract that's most often cited is Francis Bacon's *The New Atlantis*, which was published in incomplete form a year after his death. The novel depicts a perfect land containing a college named Solomon's House, where knowledge and research are employed to advance society. Robert Langdon refers to the idea that the forefathers of the U.S. were inspired by this book when he passes the Folger Shakespeare Library in Chapter 73.

Bacon's assertion that reason could improve the world struck a chord with the progressive thinkers of the eighteenth century. The printing press had created a new class keen to exchange ideas and discoveries, and they were excited by Bacon's concept of progress through rationalism, free from the restrictions of class and religion.

It's easy to see how Freemasonry fits into all this. Lodges could put these utopian ideals into practice, with members free to share ideas without the usual divisions. So, did the speculative Masons really look across the Atlantic to find a place where their utopian ideals could be realized free from the tyrannical restrictions of the old world?

Well, not quite. As outlined in the "Masonic Republic" section, not all Founding Fathers were Masons, and there were members of the fraternity on both sides of the conflict in the Revolutionary War. Plus, as you might remember from history lessons, the war was inspired as much by the British Parliament's mistreatment of its colony as by lofty utopian ideals.

Nonetheless, it can be argued that the popularity of Freemasonry in the early years of the United States had a lasting impact on the character of the new nation. The fraternity provided a framework for the spread of the enlightenment values of freedom, tolerance and opportunity. These are words that you might still hear today if you asked an American to describe their nation.

See also: Bacon, Francis; Masonic Republic.

Washington, George

Depictions of George Washington run throughout *The Lost Symbol*. At the start of the novel, Peter Solomon's severed hand points up at Constantino Brumidi's fresco *The Apotheosis of Washington*. Also in the Capitol, Robert Langdon recalls Horatio Greenough's "Washington Zeus" statue. When he's teaching his students about Freemasonry, Langdon shows them a mural of George Washington laying the cornerstone of the Capitol Building in Masonic regalia. Later on, Langdon and Katherine Solomon misdirect the CIA into thinking they're heading for the George Washington Masonic National Memorial in Alexandria. Finally, the novel concludes with the sunrise on the Washington Monument.

George Washington was the commander of the Continental Army in the American Revolutionary War, the first president of the United States of America, and the most celebrated figure in the foundation of the U.S. He is also arguably the most famous Freemason in history.

Washington's life is shrouded in legend, as might be expected for such a major figure. The man to blame for some of these myths was an Anglican minister named Mason Locke Weems, better known as Parson Weems. In the early nineteenth century, Weems published *A History of the Life and Death, Virtues and Exploits of General George Washington*, containing apocryphal tales such as the young Washington admitting to chopping down a cherry tree. This work of fan fiction passed off as biography was established as a set text for generations of American schoolchildren, embedding misconceptions that have been hard to shift.

Weems gives an account of Washington's death that involves him ascending to heaven as a saint surrounded by angels. It is this description that inspired Brumidi's *The Apotheosis of Washington*, the fresco that introduces the theme of the divinity of man into *The Lost Symbol*.

Washington was born on February 22, 1732, on his family's Pope Creek estate, which is situated near present-day Colonial Beach in Westmoreland County, Virginia. When George was eleven, his father, Augustine, died, leaving George's half brother, Lawrence Washington, to become a surrogate father and role model. Unable to afford a formal education, Washington started work as a surveyor at the age of sixteen to help support his family.

In 1752 Lawrence died of tuberculosis, and George became the owner of the family plantation. He made a success of his inheritance, eventually owning more than 8,000 acres of land across five different farms. It was also in 1752 that Washington was initiated into a Masonic lodge in Fredericksburg, and the principles of the fraternity would prove to have a lasting impact on his life.

Washington was raised to the status of Master Mason just a year later. He is thought to have retained his ties to the organization during the French and Indian War, and attended military Masonic lodges, apparently meeting in a cave near Charles Town, West Virginia, which is now known as "Washington's Masonic Cave."

When fighting broke out in the Revolutionary War in 1775, Washington was appointed commander in chief of the Continental Army. His popularity and military experience made him an obvious choice, even though he personally claimed that he wasn't equal to it.

As in the French and Indian War, Washington was involved with military Masons. He led a procession of about a hundred Masons in West Point in 1779, in celebration of the feast day of St. John the Baptist. Washington encouraged membership in military lodges, believing that Freemasonry could help soldiers from different backgrounds find common ground, and strengthen the bonds between them.

Washington's ties to the fraternity remained strong after the war. In 1788, the year before he was elected president, he became the charter master of the Alexandria Lodge, whose members now meet in the George Washington Masonic National Memorial, which features in Chapter 78 of *The Lost Symbol*. He was elected the first president of the United States of America on February 4, 1789, and took the presidential oath of office on April 30, 1789, in a ceremony administered by Robert Livingstone, the Grand Master of New York's Grand Lodge.

As Washington oversaw the formation of a new nation, his Masonic connections remained important to him. In 1793, he wore his Masonic apron at a ceremony to lay the cornerstone of the Capitol Building, which included the traditional offerings of corn, wine and oil.

Far from being a secretive front for any sinister plot, Freemasonry taught Washington to tolerate the beliefs of others. Masons refer to the Supreme Being as "The Great Architect of the Universe" not because they worship secret pagan gods as conspiracy theorists claim, but to respect the private beliefs of each member. In accordance with this, records show that Washington used the word "Jehovah" when writing to a Jewish community, and the term "Great Spirit" when addressing a delegation of Cherokees.

Washington kept his own religious beliefs private, leading many writers to suggest that he was a deist, which is to say that he believed a supreme being created the universe and the laws of nature but doesn't intervene in it. While this would strengthen the case of those who think the United States was established as a deist rather than a Christian country, there's not a lot of direct evidence. Washington didn't take Communion in church, but never explained exactly what this meant for his belief system.

Another value that Washington seems to have taken from Freemasonry was the principle of constant self-improvement. Although denied a formal education, he was committed to self-education, eventually amassing a library of more than 900 books, one of the largest in the country.

Washington retired from the presidency in 1797, and returned to his Mount Vernon plantation to devote time to farming. He caught a cold on December 12, 1799, after inspecting his farm on horseback in the freezing rain. He died two days later, possibly as a result of the bloodletting that had been used to treat the illness. His funeral was held on December 18, and included a military honor guard and a Masonic procession. Washington was buried with his Masonic apron, and a sprig of evergreen to represent the acacia plant, the Masonic symbol of immortality and resurrection.

As his funeral arrangements show, Freemasonry remained important to Washington throughout his life. But not, as alternative historians might suggest, because it was a front for his true desire to establish a New World Order, but because he believed in its values of tolerance and self-improvement.

See also: The Apotheosis of Washington; Deism; Freemasonry; The Great Architect of the Universe; The United States Capitol; Washington, D.C.; The Washington Monument.

Washington, D.C.

It was long anticipated that the third Robert Langdon novel would take place in Washington, D.C., and Dan Brown dropped hints about it in interviews as long ago as 2003.

The layout and architecture of cities are important elements of Brown's fiction, so it should come as no surprise that the capital is the setting for Robert Langdon's first adventure on U.S. soil. As Langdon tells his students in Chapter 6 of *The Lost Symbol*, the city features "ancient stuff" like temples, pyramids and crypts—in other words, all the ingredients required for the Dan Brown formula.

Dan Brown's account of Washington, D.C., seems to have been influenced by David Ovason's book *The Secret Architecture of Our Nation's Capital*. Here Ovason details the Roman, Greek and Egyptian imagery of the city, and in Chapter 3 Robert Langdon starts to notice these ancient influences as soon as he arrives and drives past the Jefferson Memorial, the Lincoln Memorial and the Washington Monument.

Ovason is interested in the influence of the Freemasons

on the history of Washington, D.C., and Langdon also ponders the city's Masonic history in Chapter 6. Some alternative historians regard Washington as the capital of the Masonic Republic of America, and it's true that the influence of the fraternity can be traced throughout its history.

The United States Capitol was originally located in Philadelphia, but an attack on that city's Independence Hall in 1783 by a group of soldiers demanding payment for their service in the war highlighted the difficultly of protecting government buildings. James Madison argued that a distinct national capital should be established. The area around the Potomac River was selected as the site for this new capital by Madison, Thomas Jefferson and Alexander Hamilton. The states of Virginia and Maryland donated the land, and George Washington picked out a diamond-shaped area of ten square miles between the Potomac's northeast shore and the northwest shore of the river's eastern branch for the Federal District.

In early 1791, he appointed the French-born architect Pierre Charles L'Enfant to devise the city plan. L'Enfant was born in Paris in 1754, and served on George Washington's staff as captain of engineers in the Revolutionary War. He settled in New York after the war, achieving some fame as a civil engineer and architect. Given his success in this field, and his connections with Washington, he was a natural choice to design the new capital city.

L'Enfant's design featured a grid of streets overlaid with wide diagonal avenues named after states of the union and grand plazas honoring notable Americans. The most famous of these diagonal avenues was Pennsylvania Avenue, connecting the president's house (which became known as "The White House" when it was painted after a fire) with the Capitol Building. Two wide "grand avenues" were to extend from the Capitol Building and president's house, which would be lined with theaters, museums and galleries. At their intersection, a huge equestrian statue of George Washington would stand, giving inspiration to both Congress and president.

Although much has been read into the layout that L'Enfant proposed, it's worth bearing in mind how much of it was dictated by the topography of the land. For example, it would make sense to place the city's two major buildings, the Capitol Building and the Presidential Palace, on hilltops close to each other, and connect them with wide avenues. Also, the grid pattern was a logical choice for the new city, as it would make the lots easier to sell to investors.

L'Enfant was by all accounts a temperamental character, and was upset when economic realities compromised his grandiose visions for the capital. When commissioners appointed by Congress asked to see his plans, L'Enfant refused to share them, even though they couldn't begin to auction off property without a map. L'Enfant wanted to realize his plans for the city as a whole, but the commissioners insisted that they should focus on the construction of federal buildings with their limited funds.

In light of L'Enfant's endless disputes with the commissioners, George Washington fired him just over a year after his appointment, but many of his ideas for the plan of the capital survived. The layout was then taken over by Andrew Ellicott, who had been working with L'Enfant as a surveyor. Ellicott revised L'Enfant's plans, with input from both Washington and Thomas Jefferson.

In 1791, construction began on this new federal city, which was named in honor of George Washington. The cornerstone of the Capitol Building was placed in 1793 in an openly Masonic ceremony. Congress held its first session in Washington in 1800, and the Organic Act of 1801 placed the territory under the control of Congress.

The Washington of the early nineteenth century wouldn't have looked much like the city of today. The National Mall was part of L'Enfant's original plan, but it wasn't until the early twentieth century that it became the familiar strip of formal parkland. In the interim, it was used as a campsite for troops during the Civil War, and part of it was even used as a depot for the Baltimore and Potomac Railroad. And while a monument to George Washington had been proposed in the L'Enfant plan, it wasn't until 1884 that the famous obelisk was actually completed.

There's a whole genre of conspiracy theory identifying secret messages in the layout of Washington, D.C., and many of these involve the Freemasons. It should be remembered before we dip into them that those Founding Fathers who were Masons, like George Washington, didn't exactly keep it quiet. As Robert Langdon tells his students in Chapter 6, George Washington presided over the cornerstone ceremony for the Capitol Building in full Masonic dress, so there wouldn't have been much need for him to hide secret symbols in the city's street plan.

Also, Langdon gets it wrong when he names Pierre Charles L'Enfant as a Mason—there is no evidence that L'Enfant was ever in the fraternity. David Ovason states that he was "probably" a Mason in *The Secret Architecture of our Nation's Capital* and follows his claim with an equally vague footnote stating it's "very likely" that he was one.

Some have claimed that George Washington's intention to set the district on an exact ten-mile square betrays the Masonic drive for reason, rationality and perfection that the new city would embody. But it's by zooming in on the street plan of Washington, D.C., that conspiracy theorists have really enjoyed themselves.

Hundreds of hidden Masonic references have been identified in the street plan by excitable conspiracy theorists. One of the most famous is the "pair of compasses" that can be traced with the Capitol Building at the top, one leg leading to the White House and the other leading to the Jefferson Memorial. If this is going to be a convincing Masonic symbol, of course, the compasses need a square to go with them. Some trace this from the White House to the Lincoln Memorial to the Jefferson Memorial, which would place the square lower than on the traditional Masonic symbol. Others create the square using Canal Street and Louisiana Avenue, although this isn't quite satisfactory either, as it makes the legs of the compass too long.

Some alarmists have even traced an inverted pentagram in the street plan above the White House. This shape has inspired frenzied speculation that far from following a Christian God, the Founding Fathers were in fact Masonic Devil worshippers. But their diabolical plan would have been slightly flawed. The shape traced along the streets is a little too wide and too short to be a satisfying pentagram. Worse, you need only to look at a map of Washington, D.C., to see that it's at best a partial pentagram, as Rhode Island Avenue doesn't quite join up with the intersection of New Hampshire Avenue and Pennsylvania Avenue. Surely if you're going to go to all the effort of concealing Satanic beliefs in a street plan, you'd do it properly.

In their book *The Temple and the Lodge*, Michael Baigent and Richard Leigh claim that the modifications made to the street plan by George Washington and Thomas Jefferson created several shapes that are similar to the insignia cross of the Knights Templar. They use this to further their case that the true roots of Freemasonry are in the medieval military order.

Ironically, the more these theories proliferate, the less convincing they become. They combine not to convince us that the Masons hid symbols in the layout of Washington, D.C., but rather that in the plan of a city based on a grid pattern with intersecting diagonal lines, you'll be able to find most of the shapes you want to find.

Langdon sensibly dismisses these theories when one of his Harvard students tells him about them in Chapter 6, but Dan Brown seems to have been more impressed with the astrological account of Washington, D.C., that David Ovason gives in *The Secret Architecture of Our Nation's Capital*. In fact, Langdon even tells his students that the Masonic cornerstone ceremonies of Washington took place while the Caput Draconis was in Virgo, which is something Ovason describes in great detail in Chapter 4 of his book. He painstakingly lists the ways in which the constellation Virgo featured in the history and design of Washington, D.C., throughout his book. He suggests that

Virgo is important to Freemasons because of its association with pre-Christian goddesses and the whole of the city can be seen as a pagan altar. Not that Freemasonry actually does place any significance on Virgo, of course.

Whether you subscribe to Langdon's mystical take on the city or not, there's no doubt that Washington, D.C., provides enough unexpected locations to make a fitting location for a Dan Brown novel. As Langdon tells his students, it can hold its own against any European city for hidden history.

See also: Freemasonry; Satanism; The United States Capitol; Washington, George; The Washington Monument.

The Washington Monument

Robert Langdon notices the Washington Monument as he flies into Washington, D.C., at the start of *The Lost Symbol*. The monument appears again at the end of the novel, when Peter Solomon blindfolds Robert Langdon and leads him up to the viewing chamber.

The Washington Monument is an obelisk made of marble, granite and sandstone, situated on the National Mall in Washington, D.C. At 555 feet, it was at one point the world's tallest structure, and it remains the tallest stone structure.

The building of a monument to George Washington was suggested in Pierre Charles L'Enfant's original city plans, but it wasn't until 1884, more than eight decades after Washington's death, that it was finally completed. The monument was designed by Robert Mills, an architect and Freemason who was appointed by the Washington National Monument Society. His original design was for a 600-foot obelisk with a flat top surrounded by a colonnade full of statues of the Founding Fathers. On top of the colonnade, Mills wanted to place a statue of

Washington riding a chariot and above the doorway the Egyptian symbol of the winged sun.

The Monument Society liked the design, but not the cost, which would have been more than a million dollars. They decided to start work on the obelisk and leave the colonnade for later, hoping that the citizens of Washington would be encouraged to donate money if they saw work commence on the monument. The monument was originally going to be placed on the spot designated by L'Enfant, where the line running directly from the center of the White House meets the line running directly from the center of the Capitol. However, the ground at this location proved unsuitable to support a structure as heavy as the planned obelisk, and the site was shifted about 100 yards southeast. According to conspiracy theorists, this shift put the monument in perfect alignment with the House of the Temple, although the alignment actually falls somewhere between 15th and 16th streets.

The cornerstone of the monument was laid in an elaborate Masonic ceremony on July 4, 1848, by Grand Master Benjamin B. French of the Grand Lodge of Free and Accepted Masons of the District of Columbia. He is said to have used the same sash, apron and gavel as Washington did for the cornerstone ceremony at the U.S. Capitol in 1793. In keeping with Masonic traditions, he poured vials of corn, wine and oil over the cornerstone.

As the Monument Society began to run short of funds, they allowed stones from around the U.S. and abroad to be donated for the monument. One of these was a marble block from the Temple of Concord in Rome donated by Pope Pius IX. This gift angered the Know-Nothings, a contemporary political movement opposed to Irish Catholic immigration. For them, the Pope's gift was evidence of the Vatican's will for world domination.

On March 6, 1854, the Pope's Stone was stolen from the grounds of the incomplete Washington Monument. Although a reward was offered, the stone was never recovered and no arrests were ever made. One account claims that the Know-Nothings dumped the stone in the Potomac River, while another claims that they ground it up and used it to make mortar in the monument.

The capstone of the Washington Monument was finally set on December 6, 1884, and the completed obelisk was dedicated on February 21 the following year. It held the title of the world's tallest structure until the completion of the Eiffel Tower in 1889.

The dominance of the Washington Monument in the layout of the nation's capital has been stressed by those who hold that the United States was founded as a Masonic republic, though claiming that a monument designed by a Mason to honor a Mason and inaugurated in a Masonic ceremony betrays the influence of the Masons hardly counts as a conspiracy theory.

The architecture of the monument has inspired many fanciful theories about the importance of ancient Egypt to the Masonic Founding Fathers. In his book *The Secret Architecture of our Nation's Capital*, David Ovason uses astrology to link the monument to ancient Egypt. He suggests that Egyptian pyramids and temples were built in alignment to Sirius, the Dog Star, which was also important to the Masonic Founding

Fathers of the United States. He claims that the Declaration of Independence was signed when the sun was in alignment with Sirius in July 1776, and that the sun passed over Sirius in 1848, when the cornerstone of the Washington Monument was laid, so that the star would have been visible over the Capitol Building during the ceremony.

As he stands at the top of the monument at the end of *The Lost Symbol*, Langdon suggests that the two circles of dark stone around the monument make it resemble the ancient symbol of the circumpunct from above, despite having dismissed theories about mystical symbols in the layout of Washington, D.C., in Chapter 6 of the novel.

As Langdon notes, the monument's aluminium capstone is inscribed on one side with the words "Laus Deo," meaning "Praise be to God," which is the phrase that the symbols on the bottom of the Masonic pyramid spell out when transliterated into the Roman alphabet. The three other sides of the capstone are also inscribed, but with details of the people involved in the monument's construction, which wouldn't make for a very exciting secret message.

See also: Pyramids and Ancient Egypt; Washington, George; Washington, D.C.

Washington National Cathedral

In Chapter 76 of *The Lost Symbol*, Robert Langdon and Katherine Solomon lead the CIA to believe that they're heading for the George Washington Masonic National Memorial while in fact traveling in the opposite direction, to Washington National Cathedral.

Washington National Cathedral is located on Mount Alban, one of the highest spots in the northwest quadrant of the city. Although Pierre Charles L'Enfant's original city plan set land aside for a "great church for national purposes" where the National Portrait Gallery now stands, it wasn't until 1907 that work began on the cathedral.

Despite the official status its name implies, Washington National Cathedral is an Episcopalian church, and was built with private donations. However, the cathedral frequently serves the national purposes that L'Enfant described. So far, it's been the location for the state funerals of Woodrow Wilson, Dwight D. Eisenhower, Ronald Reagan and Gerald Ford, as well as for presidential prayer services following the inaugurations of Franklin D. Roosevelt, Ronald Reagan, George H. W. Bush, George W. Bush and Barack Obama.

As Dean Galloway's clue in Chapter 70 suggests, the floor in front of the Jerusalem altar contains ten stones taken from Mount Sinai, the mountain in Saint Katherine City in the Sinai Peninsula of Egypt where God supposedly gave the Ten Commandments to Moses, as described in the Book of Exodus.

The stone from heaven mentioned in Dean Galloway's clue refers to the "space window," a stained-glass commemoration of the moon landings, which has a fragment of lunar rock encased in it. And, as Langdon explains to Katherine Solomon, the mention of "Luke's dark father" is a reference to the cathedral's famous Darth Vader grotesque. This carving on the high northwest tower was crafted by Jay Hall Carpenter and Patrick J. Plunkett, and was the result of a competition to design a sculpture for the cathedral held by National Geographic's *World* magazine. While not all Christians are completely comfortable with this concession to the rival religion of Sith, they should at least be thankful that the competition winner didn't choose an Ewok or Jar Jar Binks.

See also: The George Washington Masonic National Memorial; Washington, D.C.

Washington Zeus

In Chapter 21 of *The Lost Symbol*, Robert Langdon tells Director Sato that the rotunda of the Capitol Building once contained a huge sculpture of George Washington resembling the Greek god Zeus. Although the statue was built for the Capitol Building, it is now housed in the National Museum of American History on the National Mall, so Sato has to Google it on her BlackBerry.

Horatio Greenough's statue *George Washington* was commissioned in 1832. It's sometimes referred to as "Washington Zeus" or "American Zeus," as it was modeled on Phidias's sculpture of Zeus in Olympia, one of the Seven Wonders of the Ancient World. Phidias's Zeus was thirty-nine feet high and made of ivory and gold-plated bronze. The temple housing it was destroyed in the early fifth century A.D., and historians believe that the statue itself was either destroyed then or in Constantinople later in the century.

Greenough was commissioned to create a statue of Washington to mark the centenary of his birth. It was to be housed on the floor of the rotunda, directly underneath Constantino Brumidi's fresco *The Apotheosis of Washington*, which shows the president ascending to heaven as a deity. Given this placement, it's no surprise that Greenough decided to continue the divine theme, but many were uncomfortable with the image of Washington as a pagan god when it was unveiled in 1841.

The statue shows a seated Washington with his upper body naked and his lower body covered with a toga. His right arm is raised, with the index finger pointing upward to *The Apotheosis of Washington*, just as Peter Solomon's severed hand does at the start of *The Lost Symbol*. His left arm reaches outward, holding a sheathed sword.

This strange pose has inspired the conspiracy theorist and former Hereford United goalkeeper David Icke to link the statue with an illustration of Baphomet by the occultist Eliphas Lévi in his book *The Biggest Secret*: "So why portray him like that? And why was his right hand pointing up and his left hand pointing down? . . . They made the statue in the image of Baphomet of Mendes or Asmodeos, the Satanists' symbol of the 'Devil.'" For some reason, Icke regards this vague similarity as proof that Freemasons are Devil-worshippers.

The statue was placed in the rotunda in 1841, but it proved unpopular with many mid-nineteenth-century Americans, who felt Washington's nudity to be at odds with their stately image of him. It was also too heavy for a floor that, as Robert Langdon points out in Chapter 20 of *The Lost Symbol*, was built over the Capitol Crypt. When the floor began to crack in 1843, the statue was moved to the east lawn of the Capitol, where it remained until it began to show signs of weather damage. It was then relocated to the Smithsonian Castle, and finally to the National Museum of American History, where it can be seen today.

While it's a slight disappointment that the only way Greenough's bizarre statue can make an appearance in *The Lost Symbol* is on the screen of someone's BlackBerry, it's easy to see why Brown couldn't resist including in his novel the image of the first U.S. president transformed into a muscle-bound pagan god.

See also: *The Apotheosis of George Washington*; Satanism; The United States Capitol; Washington, George.

The Widow's Son

Shortly after *The Da Vinci Code* became a publishing phenomenon, many newspapers and websites ran stories about secret messages hidden on the dust jacket of the U.S. version of the book. One of these clues could be identified if you isolated the letters in the blurb printed in slightly bolder type. If you did, you found the following characters:

I S T H E R E N O H E L P F O R T H E W I D O W S S O N

To those who knew the story of Hiram Abiff, it was apparent that Langdon's next adventure would involve the Freemasons. In the legend, which is central to many of the symbols and rituals of Freemasonry, Hiram Abiff was the architect appointed to oversee the building of King Solomon's Temple on Mount Moriah, the place now known as Temple Mount. He is called the "widow's son" because the worker named as Hiram is described this way in the First Book of Kings:

And King Solomon sent and fetched Hiram out of Tyre.

He was a widow's son of the tribe of Naphtali, and his father was a man of Tyre, a worker in brass: and he was filled with wisdom, and understanding, and cunning to work all works in brass. And he came to king Solomon, and wrought all his work.

(I KINGS 7:13–14)

In the Masonic account, which differs from the biblical one, three of the workers on the Temple of Solomon are said to have murdered Hiram Abiff when he refused to reveal the secrets of the craft and raise them to the rank of Master Mason. Abiff's last words before he died were apparently "Is there no help for the widow's son?" The question is still used as an encoded request for help from fellow Masons.

As anticipated, the question is used in this way in *The Lost Symbol*. Warren Bellamy asks it of Dean Galloway, who then gives Robert Langdon and Katherine Solomon sanctuary at the Washington National Cathedral. The phrase "widow's son" is also used in the reenactment of the Hiram Abiff story that Mal'akh secretly records.

In accordance with the tradition of dust-jacket clues, there are several codes on the dust jacket of the U.S. version of *The Lost Symbol* that might relate to the content of the next Robert Langdon novel. On the back cover, there are a couple of lines in Masonic cipher which can be translated as "All great truths begin as blasphemies," a quotation from George Bernard Shaw's 1918 play *Annajanska, the Bolshevik Empress*. This quotation has relevance to Brown's favorable portrayal of

Noetic Science in *The Lost Symbol*, as in Chapter 84 Dean Galloway compares skepticism about Katherine's work to mankind's previous refusal to believe that the world was round. It might also point to the content of the next novel. Could this clue, together with the reference to St. Petersburg's Hermitage Museum in Chapter 5, imply that the next book has a Russian setting?

Also on the back cover are sixteen letters arranged in a 4 x 4 grid:

Y U O E
M S T D
I I N H
R E K Y

These letters can be rearranged according to the magic square from Dürer's *Melencolia I*:

16	3	2	13
5	10	11	8
9	6	7	12
4	15	14	1

Using Dürer's square as a transposition cipher gives:

Y O U R
M I N D
I S T H
E K E Y

The phrase "Your mind is the key" has clear relevance to the Noetic idea explored in *The Lost Symbol* that thought can change the world, but we'll have to wait and see if it also has relevance to the next Langdon book.

On the front cover of the U.S. hardcover edition, there are two groups of numbers printed around the faint red circle that surrounds the Masonic seal. The first group reads "22 65 22 97 27" and the second "22 23 44 1 133 97 65 44." The fact that the largest of these numbers is 133 is a clue that this code refers to the chapters of *The Lost Symbol*. Taking the first letter of each corresponding chapter gives the phrase "Popes Pantheon." This could imply that Catholicism will figure again in the next Langdon adventure, although some fans have linked it to the Jefferson Memorial, described as "America's Pantheon" in Chapter 3 of *The Lost Symbol*, which was designed by John Russell Pope.

Finally, there are a few combinations of letters and numbers hidden around the cover that give A2 B1 C2 D7 E8 F2 G9 H5 I1 J5, producing a New York phone number, 212 782 9515. The first thirty-three people to crack the code and call this number received a signed copy of *The Lost Symbol*.

See also: Freemasonry; *Kryptos*; Noetic Science; Solomon's Temple.

APPENDIX

THE SYMBOLS ON THE MASONIC PYRAMID

In Chapter 101 of *The Lost Symbol*, we find that the base of the Masonic pyramid is covered with carvings of symbols that were concealed with wax and stone dust. When reordered according to the numbers on an order-eight magic square devised by Benjamin Franklin, they create the word "Heredom" (which is said to mean "holy house" and identified as a code word for the House of the Temple), a large pyramid, a winding staircase and five distinct groups of symbols. This appendix gives an overview of these symbols, but note that some of them appear in the Symbol Quest game on Dan Brown's website, so you might want to skip this section until you've played the game.

The Pyramid

Several of the diagonal lines inscribed on the original array of symbols combine to create a large pyramid after reordering. Here, as elsewhere in the novel, the pyramid is used as a symbol for the lost wisdom of the ancients (*see* Pyramids and Ancient Egypt).

The Winding Staircase

The winding staircase is a symbol used in the second degree of Freemasonry, Fellow Craft, where it represents the journey into the middle chamber of Solomon's Temple, inspired by the reference to a stairway in the First Book of Kings in the Bible.

As Robert Langdon suggests, the winding staircase sometimes appears on Masonic tracing boards, which are canvases or boards covered with the symbols associated with a particular degree ceremony. The tradition developed from eighteenth-century meetings at which, forbidden from transcribing ritual in a way that nonmembers could understand, Masons would print symbols on a cloth and hang it over an easel. Several other symbols from these boards appear on either side of the pyramid, as described below.

THE SECOND ROW

The second row of the grid, underneath the line that spells out the word "Heredom," is made up of the symbols for the seven planets known to the ancients (the sun and the moon were regarded as planets then). In alchemy, each of the planets was said to rule a particular metal, so these symbols also came to stand for the seven planetary metals.

Saturn

This symbol represents the scythe of Saturn, the Roman god of harvest. In alchemy, it's associated with lead. In the Symbol Quest game, it's the answer to the clue "Scribe of Sidereus Nuncius was the first to see rings around it," a reference to a treatise published by Galileo Galilei in 1610.

Mars

This symbol represents the shield and spear of Mars, the Roman god of war. In alchemy, it's associated with iron.

It's also the symbol used to represent the male sex. In the Symbol Quest game, it's the answer to the clue "Fourth rock from the sun."

Mercury

This symbol represents the staff and winged helmet of Mercury, the Roman god of commerce. In alchemy, it's associated with the metal mercury. In the Symbol Quest game on Dan Brown's website, it's the answer to the clue "Quicksilver."

The Sun

This symbol crops up a lot in the novel, and is discussed in the section "Circumpunct." As well as representing the sun, it's associated with gold in alchemy.

The Moon

This is the symbol of the crescent moon. In alchemy, it's associated with silver.

Venus

This symbol represents the hand mirror of Venus, the Roman goddess of love. In alchemy it's associated with copper. It is also the symbol used to represent the female sex. In the Symbol Quest game, it's the answer to the clue "Venus's hand mirror."

$$24$$

Jupiter

The symbol represents the thunderbolt of Jupiter, the king of the Roman gods. In alchemy, it's associated with tin.

THE THIRD ROW

As well as containing the capstone of the pyramid, the third row of the grid includes six symbols that are transliterated into the Roman alphabet as "Laus Deo," the letters inscribed on one side of the capstone of the Washington Monument.

The Square
This famous Masonic symbol stands for honesty, truth and virtue, and is combined with the compasses to create the emblem of the fraternity.

Au

Au
Au is the chemical symbol for gold, which appears in the d-block of the Periodic Table of the Elements. Like many chemical symbols, it was assigned according to the element's Latin name, "aurum."

Sigma
Sigma is the eighteenth letter of the Greek alphabet, and carries the "s" sound. It's used as the symbol of summation in mathematics.

Delta

Delta is the letter "D" in the Greek alphabet, and, as Robert Langdon notes, is also the mathematical symbol for change. In conspiracy theory, it's been linked to the triangle around the All-Seeing-Eye on the Great Seal of the United States as proof that the Illuminati intend to bring about worldwide change and establish a New World Order (*see* The Great Seal of the United States).

Mercury

This was associated with mercury in alchemy, although the third symbol of the grid's second row, which is described above, was more common.

The Ouroboros

The Ouroboros is the symbol of a snake or dragon swallowing the end of its own tail to create a circle. The symbol has been traced to ancient Egypt and Greece, and also appears in Hindu and Norse mythology. It's been associated with many ideas, such as the cyclical nature of time, the cycle of rebirth and the aspiration to a state of being beyond the material world. In *The Lost Symbol*, Mal'akh has the Ouroboros tattooed onto the top of his head, enclosing the patch of flesh on which he intends to tattoo the lost word.

AROUND THE PYRAMID

On either side of the large pyramid are a number of symbols commonly found on Masonic tracing boards.

The Five-Pointed Star

The emblem represents the Supreme Being, and corresponds to a part of the Master Mason degree known as the Five Points of Fellowship. It is an important symbol for Freemasons, as well as the Order of the Eastern Star, the Masonic-style organization women can join mentioned by Robert Langdon in Chapter 6. Conspiracy theorists have used the five-pointed star to associate the Masons with everything from the U.S. flag to Rosslyn Chapel.

The Sun and the Moon

Next to the five-pointed star are representations of the sun and moon that might be seen on a Masonic tracing board. Like the circumpunct, they represent the Supreme Being, whom they obey.

The Three Candles

On Masonic tracing boards, three burning candles are often shown in a triangular formation on the altar to represent the three "lesser lights" of the sun, moon and lodge master. They remind the master to govern the lodge with the same regularity that the sun governs the day and the moon governs the night. In Chapter 81 of *The Lost Symbol*, Mal'akh works by the light of three candles in his basement.

The Compasses

This well-known Masonic symbol represents the values of friendship, morality and restraint. In the Symbol Quest game on Dan Brown's website, a pair of compasses appears with a square and a letter G, and is the answer to the clue "Casanova, Mozart and Houdini had this in common," a reference to three of history's most famous Masons. In Freemasonry, the letter G stands for the Great Architect of the Universe, as well as geometry, which operative Masons employed in the building of large structures.

The Ashlar

This symbol represents a smooth building block. It's often seen on Masonic tracing boards alongside a rough building block. The rough ashlar symbolizes man in his imperfect state, whereas the smooth ashlar symbolizes the state he can achieve through education, faith and discipline.

The Pythagorean Theorem

At the bottom right-hand corner of the pyramid is another symbol found on Masonic tracing boards, which represents the Pythagorean Theorem. As you might remember from math lessons, the theorem states that in any right-angle triangle the square on the hypotenuse is equal to the sum of the squares on the other two sides, which was an important equation for early stonemasons. In Freemasonry, it's referred to as the 47th Problem of Euclid.

As the symbol appears inside the pyramid, which contains the symbols of the great faiths and religions, it also stands for Pythagoreanism, the brotherhood based on the teachings of Pythagoras.

INSIDE THE PYRAMID

When Robert Langdon is analyzing the symbols of the Masonic pyramid, he notes that the ones associated with the major religions are placed inside the pyramid, as if fusing together and rising toward the circumpunct. There are twelve symbols inside the pyramid, some of which will be very familiar.

The Latin Cross

The Latin Cross, or Christian Cross, is the symbol of Christianity. It becomes known as a "crucifix" when a representation of the body of Christ appears on it. In Chapter 85 of *The Lost Symbol*, Robert Langdon interprets a Latin Cross with a circumpunct in the middle as a Rosicrucian symbol (*see* The Rosicrucians).

The Star of David

The hexagram created by two equilateral triangles is a complex symbol with meaning for many different traditions, but here it's used as the Star of David or Magen David, the symbol of the Jewish faith. In *The Lost Symbol*, Katherine traces this shape over the Great Seal of the United States to form the letters in the word "Mason" (*see* page 5 of the plates section).

The Eye of Horus

The eye of the falcon god Horus was an ancient Egyptian symbol of protection, and appeared on items of jewelry such as amulets. The symbol also sometimes appeared on coffins to allow the dead to see the way ahead. It is made from seven different hieroglyphs related to the human body, and in the Symbol Quest game on Dan Brown's website it's the answer to the clue "Hieroglyph of seven body parts in one."

The Star and Crescent

The symbol of a crescent moon and star was found widely across the ancient world, although it's now mainly associated with Islam. Several theories have been suggested as to how the symbol became associated with Islam, one of which is that Ottoman Turks adopted it from the Byzantines.

Yin-Yang

The yin-yang symbol is formed by an S-shape dividing a circle into two identical shapes that are usually shown in opposing colors. Inside the shapes are dots that represent the harmony between apparently opposing forces. It's used here to represent the Chinese philosophical and religious tradition of Taoism. In the Symbol Quest game, it's the answer to the clue "Opposing, yet unified."

The Ankh

The Ankh was the Egyptian hieroglyph for "life." It was also associated with concepts such as the afterlife, the sun coming over the horizon and the union of heaven and earth. The symbol appears on either side of Robert Langdon's name on his website, perhaps as an indication that it will feature prominently in a future novel. In the Symbol Quest game, it's the answer to the clue "Robert Langdon's favorite symbol."

Ahimsa

Although the hand has many different symbolic meanings, it's probably included on the pyramid to signify Jainism, an ancient Indian religion that prescribes a path of nonviolence. The hand symbolizes Ahimsa, the rule of conduct that forbids the killing or injuring of a living being.

The Triquetra

The Triquetra is a symbol that was found in northern European runic inscriptions and in Celtic art. Today it's often associated with Neopaganism and New Age beliefs.

Aum

This symbol shows Aum, a sacred syllable in Hinduism, which is used as a mantra and in affirmations and blessings. It's the answer to the clue "Meditative chant" in the Symbol Quest game.

The Dharmachakra

The Dharmachakra is a wheel representing dharma, the path to enlightenment in Buddhism. The wheel's eight spokes relate to the Noble Eightfold Path, one of the principal teachings of Buddha.

The Pentagram

The Pentagram is the shape of a five-pointed star formed by five intersecting lines. It has meaning for many different cultures and traditions, and in *The Da Vinci Code* Robert Langdon connected it to the sacred feminine. The appearance of a circumscribed pentagram here is probably intended to represent Neopagan religions such as Wicca.

BENEATH THE PYRAMID

On either side of the winding stairway are the twelve signs of the zodiac, which correspond with twelve constellations of stars that some believe are linked to different personality types. In *The Lost Symbol*, Robert Langdon says the zodiac signs stand for the earliest religious beliefs of man. This reflects the conjectures of esoteric author Manly P. Hall, who claims in *The Secret Teachings of All Ages* that the zodiac is more than five million years old and can be traced to Atlantean civilization. The historical evidence suggests that the zodiac we know actually developed from concepts in Hellenistic and Babylonian astronomy.

Aries

This symbol represents the horns of a ram.

Taurus

This symbol represents the head and horns of a bull.

Gemini

This symbol is seen as the Roman numeral two. The constellation was interpreted by many different astrological disciplines as showing two individuals.

Cancer

Some see this symbol as representing the claws of a crab, while others have linked it to the Ouroboros.

Leo

This symbol is taken to show the head or mane of a lion.

Virgo

This symbol is sometimes interpreted as the arms of a maiden, while others have seen its overlapping tail as a sign of sexual restraint. In the Symbol Quest game on Dan Brown's website, it's the answer to the clue "Leo's chaste neighbor."

Libra

Some have associated this symbol with a setting or rising sun and the balance of day and night, while others relate it to the "equal" sign in mathematics.

Scorpio

This symbol is often taken to show the legs and tail of a scorpion. It's sometimes contrasted with the Virgo symbol as a sign of sexual energy.

Sagittarius

This symbol shows the bow and arrow of the archer. In the Symbol Quest game, it's the answer to the clue "Centaur archer."

Capricorn

This symbol is sometimes interpreted as the horn of a goat, while others link it with the tail of a fish.

Aquarius

The wavy lines of this symbol represent water. In the Symbol Quest game, it's the answer to the clue "An age in the hair of Broadway."

Pisces

This symbol is traditionally linked to the image of two fish swimming in opposite directions yet tied together.

BIBLIOGRAPHY

Anderson, James: *The Constitutions of the Free-Masons* (Kessinger Publishing, 2004)

Aubrey, John: *Brief Lives* (Boydell Press, 2009)

Baigent, Michael, and Leigh, Richard: *The Temple and the Lodge: Inside Freemasonry* (Arrow Books, 2006)

Bauval, Robert, and Hancock, Graham: *Talisman: Sacred Cities, Secret Faith* (Michael Joseph, 2004)

Bullock, Steven C.: *Revolutionary Brotherhood: Freemasonry and the Transformation of the American Social Order* (University of North Carolina Press, 1998)

Campbell, Joseph: *The Hero with a Thousand Faces* (New World Library, 2008)

Capra, Fritjof: *The Tao of Physics: An Exploration of the Parallels Between Modern Physics and Eastern Mysticism* (Flamingo, 1992)

BIBLIOGRAPHY

Chopra, Deepak: *Quantum Healing: Exploring the Frontiers of Mind / Body Medicine* (Bantam Books, 1989)

Cooper, Robert L. D.: *The Rosslyn Hoax* (Lewis Masonic, 2006)

Ellis, Joseph J.: *Founding Brothers: The Revolutionary Generation* (Vintage Books, 2002)

Gardner, Laurence: *The Shadow of Solomon* (Harper Element, 2005)

Getler, Warren, and Brewer, Bob: *Shadow of the Sentinel: One Man's Quest to Find the Hidden Treasure of the Confederacy* (Simon & Schuster, 2003)

Hall, Manly P.: *Freemasonry of the Ancient Egyptians* (Philosophical Research Society, 1982)

Hall, Manly P.: *The Secret Destiny of America* (Jeremy P. Tarcher, 2008)

Hall, Manly P.: *The Secret Teachings of All Ages* (Gerald Duckworth, 2007)

Holmes, David L.: *The Faiths of the Founding Fathers* (OUP U.S.A., 2006)

Jacob, Margaret C.: *The Origins of Freemasonry: Facts and Fictions* (University of Pennsylvania Press, 2005)

Jeffers, H. Paul: *Freemasons: Inside the World's Oldest Secret Society* (Citadel Press, 2005)

Knight, Christopher, and Lomas, Robert: *The Hiram Key: Pharaohs, Freemasons and the Discovery of the Secret Scrolls of Christ* (Arrow Books, 1997)

Knight, Christopher, and Lomas, Robert: *The Second Messiah: Templars, the Turin Shroud and the Great Secret of Freemasonry* (Arrow Books, 1998)

Lee Brown, Walter: *A Life of Albert Pike* (University of Arkansas Press, 1997)

Lomas, Robert: *The Invisible College* (Corgi Books, 2009)

Lomas, Robert: *The Secret Science of Masonic Initiation* (Lewis Masonic, 2008)

Lomas, Robert: *The Secrets of Freemasonry: Revealing the Suppressed Tradition* (Robinson, 2009)

Mackey, Albert: *The History of Freemasonry: Its Legendary Origins* (Dover, 2009)

McTaggart, Lynne: *The Field* (Harper Element, 2001)

McTaggart, Lynne: *The Intention Experiment: Use your Thoughts to Change the World* (Harper Element, 2007)

Manuel, Frank E.: *Portrait of Isaac Newton* (Muller, 1980)

Mindell, Arthur: *Quantum Mind and Healing: How to Listen and Respond to Your Body's Symptoms* (Hampton Roads Publishing, 2004)

Ovason, David: *The Secret Architecture of Our Nation's Capital: The Masons and the Building of Washington, D.C.* (HarperCollins, 2002)

Oxbrow, Mark, and Robertson, Ian: *Rosslyn and the Grail* (Mainstream Publishing, 2006)

Payson, Seth: *Proof of the Illuminati* (Invisible College Press, 2003)

Pickett, Lynn, and Prince, Clive: *The Templar Revelation: Secret Guardians of the True Identity of Christ* (Corgi, 2007)

Pickover, Clifford A.: *The Zen of Magic Squares, Circles and Stars: An Exhibition of Surprising Structures across Dimensions* (Princeton University Press, 2003)

Pike, Albert: *Morals and Dogma of the Ancient and Accepted Rite of Freemasonry* (Standard Publications, 2007)

Schlitz, Marilyn, and Vieten, Cassandra: *Living Deeply: The Art and Science of Transformation in Everyday Life* (New Harbinger, 2008)

Schlitz, Marilyn, Amorok, Tina, and Micozzi, Marc S.: *Consciousness and Healing: Integrated Approaches to Mind-Body Medicine* (Churchill Livingstone, 2005)

Schnoebelen, William: *Masonry: Beyond the Light* (Chick Publications, 1991)

Stavish, Mark: *Freemasonry: Rituals, Symbols and History of the Secret Society* (Llewellyn Publications, 2007)

Talbot, Michael: *The Holographic Universe* (HarperCollins, 1996)

Tresidder, Jack: *The Watkins Dictionary of Symbols* (Duncan Baird Publishers, 1999)

Tulbure, Solomon: *The Illuminati Manifesto* (iUniverse, 2001)

Waite, Arthur Edward: *The Mysteries of Magic: A Digest of the Writings of Eliphas Lévi* (Adamant Media Corporation, 2000)

Williamson, George Hunt: *Other Tongues, Other Flesh* (BiblioBazaar, 2008)

Yates, Frances A.: *The Rosicrucian Enlightenment* (Routledge, 2001)

Young, John K.: *Sacred Sites of the Knights Templar* (Fair Winds Press, 2005)

Zukav, Gary: *The Dancing Wu Li Masters* (HarperOne, 2001)

PICTURE CREDITS

PICTURE CREDITS

ABOUT THE AUTHOR

Tim Collins lives and works in London. He is the author of several books and has contributed to many magazines and newspapers. He is not a member of the Freemasons, and only very rarely drinks wine from a human skull.